ARTIFICIAL INTELLIGENCE
THEORY, LOGIC AND APPLICATION

ARTIFICIAL INTELLIGENCE
THEORY, LOGIC AND APPLICATION

JAMES F. BRULÉ

TAB BOOKS Inc.
Blue Ridge Summit, PA 17214

FIRST EDITION
FIRST PRINTING

Copyright © 1986 by TAB BOOKS Inc.
Printed in the United States of America

Library of Congress Cataloging in Publication Data

Brulé, James F.
Artificial intelligence.

Bibliography: p.
Includes index.
1. Artificial intelligence. I. Title.
Q335.B78   1986   006.3   86-5840
ISBN 0-8306-0371-9
ISBN 0-8306-0471-5 (pbk.)

Contents

ARTIFICIAL INTELLIGENCE
THEORY, LOGIC AND APPLICATION

Introduction

For many years, computer scientists have been pursuing a line of research that has appeared arcane to some, frightening to others, and incomprehensible to many more: they have been involved in the pursuit of *artificial intelligence*. Now, at last, the everyday person is beginning to see the first practical outgrowths of this research.

The business world—the primary recipient of these applications—has yet to develop a consensus of opinion about this new technology. Some quarters detect the first signs of major change in the ways that computers will, and can, be used, and are rushing quickly towards the new products and techniques. More cautious groups, perhaps equally aware of the scope of the changes soon to be forthcoming, are patiently waiting, allowing others to take the associated risks. Most, though, feel the vague uncertainty that comes from knowing that something important is taking place, but not knowing how to proceed or even what direction to go in.

It is for the open-minded but as yet uninformed business person that this book is intended: it is a guide to the world of artificial intelligence and its application to the real world of business; it shows the simplicity behind many of the mysteries and the depths to be plumbed beneath some of the most innocent-appearing problems.

The book takes a three-pronged approach, beginning with theoretical issues, moving from there into some of the "nuts and bolts" of AI, and finally going into the world of present-day applications.

The theoretical section begins with an introduction to artificial intelligence from a generalist's point of view, starting with the underpinnings of artificial intelligence. This section includes a historical overview (Chapter 1), some theoretic structures (Chapter 2), and a study of the methods of knowledge representation (Chapter 3).

The "hard core" issues of logical approaches to AI are addressed next. This section looks at the methods of graph search (Chapter 4), the various programming languages for artificial intelligence (Chapter 5), problem-solving techniques (Chapter 6), and pattern recognition techniques (Chapter 7).

Finally, the world of expert systems is examined, from a broad perspective at first (Chapter 8) and then through the examination of some current applications (Chapter 9).

Throughout this book, programming examples and real-world applications are presented to give a solid grounding in what is possible to accomplish and what is unlikely. Moreover, after completing this text, you should be able to judge on a more objective basis the claims being made for—and against—the introduction of artificial intelligence techniques into the business world.

Thanks go to John Grey for suggesting my move into the world of publishing; to Bill Dunkerly for seeing the potential of this book; to Ginnie and Clarke Greene for their encouragement before I even knew I would be writing it; to Sandy Blount for reminding me that there were even more exciting things to be done, if only I would finish; and to my family, especially my wife Jill, for their patience and quiet support.

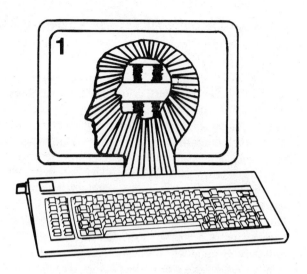

The History of Artificial Intelligence

The first question that arises when the field of artificial intelligence is addressed is, "What is it?" For most people the words conjure up notions of disembodied brains, residing in computers, or of human-appearing robots, posed either to assist humanity or dethrone them. And perhaps the dreams that seeded the original efforts in this area were not unlike these visions. In the years that have followed, however, artificial intelligence has come to denote a breadth of study that is so wide that it is difficult to call it a single field anymore. Recently, David Waltz categorized the articles claiming to be about AI for a company called Scientific DataLink, and he arrived at 13 major topic areas (Waltz, 1985). Between these 13 categories and their subsections, there are over 475 different topics, all associated with the generic term *artificial intelligence*. Thus it is no wonder that its definition has grown increasingly fuzzy.

In this chapter we will first address the classic area of AI, that of simulating human intelligence, as proposed by Alan Turing. Two programs that have done quite well at demonstrating AI, according to Turing's standards, will be explored. These programs, known as *Eliza* and *Parry*, were products of the 1960s and 70s, and represent what might be called a *conversational* approach to AI. Next more modern systems will be examined, notably *Prospector* and *Mycin*, which fall into the *expert system* category. Finally, an overview of the broad areas of AI identified by Waltz will be presented as a thumbnail guide to this growing field.

THE TURING TEST

The first person to address the problem of artificial intelligence in a practical sense was Alan Turing, a brilliant mathematician who worked for the British Ministry of Defense during the Second World War at their highly successful decoding effort. He is noted, among other things, for his work in a branch of mathematics known as finite state automata. As a thought experiment, he proposed a type of computer whose utility survives to this day; it is known as the *Turing machine.*

In 1950 Turing proposed a pragmatic test for artificial intelligence that has become known by his name: the *Turing test*. It was published in the journal *Mind* under the title "Computing Machinery and Intelligence" and is regarded as a classic in the field.

Turing's goal was to develop a test for computers that could be used to establish whether or not they were intelligent, using average people as judges. He based his test on a parlor game of the time, which was played as follows: two guests, one male and the other female, were hidden in two separate rooms. A third person, known as the judge, was located in a third room, out of sight or sound of the two guests. The judge's task was to determine which of the two guests was the woman, based entirely on notes passed between the judge and the two guests. The woman was to try and convince the judge that she was the woman, as was the man. The winner was the guest who succeeded in getting the judge to pick him or her as the woman.

The variation on this game proposed by Turing was to have one human and one machine "guest," each of whom communicated with the "judge" via a teletype. Both the human and the machine would be trying to convince the judge that "they" were human, and that the other was the machine. If the judge picked the machine or could not decide. then, Turing asserted, the machine had demonstrated intelligence. Turing was not concerned with whether the machine was "actually" intelligent, preferring not to delve into that particular philosophical morass; instead, he simply stated that for all practical purposes, the machine was performing as if it were intelligent, and that was sufficient.

By the year 2000, Turing suggested, a machine would pass his test, and it appears as though he may prove to be accurate in his prediction. While no program has yet to "pass" the complete Turing test—that is, to survive a challenge in which the judge is actively trying to determine which participant is human, and the human is aware that there is a nonhuman competitor—a number of systems have attempted to come close.

ELIZA: THE FIRST COMPUTER PSYCHIATRIST

The first and perhaps most widely known system to be subjected to a modified Turing test was a program known as Eliza, available now in a variety of forms for personal computers. Written by Joseph Weizenbaum at M.I.T. in the mid 1960s, Eliza mimicked the conversational style of a Rogerian psychotherapist. Its "test" consisted of making it available to a number of college students, who were free to "converse" with it for as long as they desired. The control group consisted of another group of students who communicated with an actual psychotherapist, also by teletype. At the end of their sessions with each, the students were asked if they had been communicating with a person or a program. A surprising percentage of the students who had been "talking" with Eliza not only thought that they had been in contact with a person, but refused to believe that it was a program, and requested further sessions with it.

Here is a typical conversation with Eliza (Eliza's responses are in capitals):

** Men are all alike.

IN WHAT WAYS

** They're always bugging us about something or other.

CAN YOU THINK OF A SPECIFIC EXAMPLE

** Well, my boyfriend made me come here.

YOUR BOYFRIEND MADE YOU COME HERE

** He says I'm depressed much of the time.

I AM SORRY TO HEAR THAT YOU ARE DEPRESSED.

** It's true. I'm unhappy.

DO YOU THINK COMING HERE WILL HELP YOU NOT TO BE UNHAPPY

** I need some help, that much seems certain.

WHAT WOULD IT MEAN TO YOU IF YOU GOT SOME HELP

** Perhaps I could learn to get along with my mother.

TELL ME MORE ABOUT YOUR FAMILY

- •
- •
- •

WHAT ELSE COMES TO YOUR MIND WHEN YOU THINK OF
YOUR FATHER

** Bullies.

DOES THAT HAVE ANYTHING TO DO WITH THE FACT
THAT YOUR BOYFRIEND MADE YOU COME HERE

- •
- •
- •

Eliza was a very simple program: it retained only a minimum of "knowledge" about the topics presented to it by the student, and in fact it accomplished most of its "conversation" by making simple grammatical changes
and reflecting the student's statement back to him or her. In this respect,
it was an elegant solution to the problem of creating human conversation.

It was not, however, a true case of the Turing test, for two reasons:
first, the students communicated only with a person or Eliza, not both in
tandem. Further, and more importantly, the students were not informed
in advance that they might be communicating with a computer, and that
they should be making efforts in their conversation to try and determine
the true nature of their correspondent. Nonetheless, Eliza's performance
was impressive; in fact, once "her" existence was known throughout the
student body, the drain on computing resources caused by the large numbers
of people running the program eventually resulted in its being removed from
the system.

PARRY: THE FIRST COMPUTERIZED PSYCHIATRIC PATIENT

A second system, also based on a psychiatric interaction, came closer
to a true Turing test, and managed to convince a significant proportion of
its subjects that it was human. Known as *Parry* (short for Paranoid
Schizophrenic), this system took the part of the patient, rather than the
therapist, in the clinical world.

Parry, developed at Stanford University by a team of researchers, was
first interviewed by eight psychiatrists live, and 33 others reviewed the
transcripts of the sessions. The reports of the 41 psychiatrists indicated that
Parry did indeed qualify as a paranoid schizophrenic. Then the same set
of psychiatrists, along with a group of 67 computer scientists, reviewed
Parry's transcript in tandem with an interview between a psychiatrist and
a human also diagnosed as paranoid schizophrenic, with the explicit goal
of determining which was the interview with the human, and which with
the computer. Only 51 percent of the psychiatrists and 48 percent of the

computer scientists could correctly identify Parry, a result no better than chance.

A typical consultation with Parry proceeded as below (Parry's portion is in capitals). Notice the difference in the quality of the dialogue as compared with Eliza:

** What do you do for a living?

I WORK AT SEARS.

** How much do you get paid an hour?

MY SALARY IS NONE OF YOUR BUSINESS.

> •
> •
> •

** What about the bookies?

A BOOKIE DIDN'T PAY ME OFF ONCE.

** And then what happened?

I HAD AN ARGUMENT WITH A BOOKIE WHO DID NOT PAY OFF. LATER ON I REMEMBERED HE HAD FRIENDS IN THE UNDERWORLD AND I THOUGHT HE WOULD USE THEM TO GET EVEN WITH ME.

** I find you interesting.

ARE YOU TRYING TO SAY SOMETHING?

> •
> •
> •

** You appear to be very sick. How do you feel right now?

I AM PERFECTLY FINE.

** Do you need to have psychiatric treatment?

I DON'T WANT TO TALK ABOUT IT.

- •
- •
- •

There may be many reasons why Parry did so well. Most importantly Parry, unlike Eliza, was based on a theory of human interaction; furthermore, Parry kept track of the conversation with the psychiatrist, if only at the simplest of levels. Parry would "open up" to the psychiatrist based on how the psychiatrist had been treating "him" in the session: if the psychiatrist had been critical or overly concerned with medications, Parry would retreat further and further from open conversation. If, however, the psychiatrist showed interest in Parry without being threatening, Parry would reveal more and more of his bizarre interpretation of the world.

Parry's performance, while excellent, was still only a limited version of the Turing test, in that the interviewers were not trying to distinguish between a human and a computer; instead, their task at the time had been to generate a diagnosis for the "person" with whom they were communicating. Nonetheless, it was an excellent example of computer-generated conversation, and it certainly lends credence to the notion that a computer program will pass the full Turing test sometime before the year 2000.

TEN YEARS LATER: EXPERT SYSTEMS

Currently the leading edge of commercially useful AI systems is in what is known as the field of *expert systems*: programs that mimic the advice-giving capabilities of human experts. Unlike their conversational predecessors, these systems make no effort to disguise the fact that they are programs, although the best do communicate in what has become known as *natural language*, language closely resembling the language of the user. The purpose of these systems is to distribute the expertise of a human expert or team of experts across a wider base than would be possible by merely using humans; with an expert system, an expert can be available to every user simply by starting up the program.

The first expert systems to become widely publicized were Prospector and Mycin; both represented fairly successful efforts at capturing and later delivering human expertise. Each used a different approach to the problems involved in trying to capture, process, and utilize human expertise; these details will be discussed further in the final chapter. For now, the discussion centers on their appearance to the user.

PROSPECTOR: A SUCCESSFUL EXPERT SYSTEM

Prospector was a system developed in 1978 for use in the petroleum industry by the team of Duda, Hart, and Reboh. Its goal was to help predict the likelihood of finding certain types of mineral deposits and geological structures, given limited information about the geology of the region. Prospector accurately predicted a large molybdenum deposit and gained instant recognition; its performance since that time, however, has been less publicized, owing either to its mediocre results or to the highly proprietary nature of the investigations that it is being used to pursue.

A typical consultation with PROSPECTOR is presented below (PROSPECTOR's dialogue is in capitals):

** There is quartz monzonite

QUARTZ MONZONITE (5)

** There is a cretaceous dike

CRETACEOUS DIKE (5)

** There is sericite and pyrite

SERICITE (5) PYRITE (5)

** There may be biotite

BIOTITE (2)

** Done

•

•

•

PRESENTLY, THE MODELS IN PROSPECTOR AND THEIR SCORES ARE:
1. KOMATIITIC NICKEL SULFIDE DEPOSIT — KNSD (0.0)
2. TYPE-A PORPHYRY COPPER DEPOSIT — PCDA (0.0)
   + + CURRENT HYPOTHESIS + +
3. KUROKO-TYPE MASSIVE SULFIDE DEPOSIT — MSD (0.001999)
4. WESTERN-STATES-TYPE SANDSTONE URANIUM DEPOSIT — WSSU (0.0)
5. MISSISSIPPI-VALLEY-TYPE LEAD/ZINC DEPOSIT — MVTD (−4.8)
WHICH OF THE ABOVE WOULD YOU LIKE TO RULE OUT?

** None

•

- •
- •
- •

THE FOLLOWING QUESTIONS ARE INTENDED TO DETER-
MINE THE NATURE OF THE REGIONAL ENVIRONMENT.

2—TO WHAT DEGREE DO YOU BELIEVE THAT:
(THERE ARE GRANITIC INTRUSIVES IN THE REGION)?

** 5

3—TO WHAT DEGREE DO YOU BELIEVE THAT:
(THE REGION CONTAINS AN ABUNDANCE OF SMALL
STOCKS)?

** −3

8—TO WHAT DEGREE DO YOU BELIEVE THAT:
(INGENIOUS ROCKS IN THE REGION HAVE PORPHYRITIC
TEXTURE)?

** Why

I AM TRYING TO ESTABLISH WHETHER SOME OF THE IN-
TRUSIVE ROCKS IN YOUR AREA HAVE TEXTURES SUG-
GESTIVE OF A HYPABYSSAL TO SUBVOLCANIC
ENVIRONMENT. PORPHYRY TEXTURES RESULTING FROM
THE RAPID COOLING AND CRYSTALLIZATION OF A
SILICATE MELT WHICH CONTAINS LARGE MINERAL
GRAINS ARE SUGGESTIVE OF RELATIVELY SHALLOW
LEVELS OF EMPLACEMENT.

- •
- •
- •

ON A SCALE FROM −5 TO 5, MY CERTAINTY THAT (THERE
ARE ALTERATION ZONES THAT ARE FAVORABLE FOR A
TYPE-A PORPHYRY COPPER DEPOSIT) IS NOW 4.833

THERE ARE TWO FAVORABLE FACTORS; IN ORDER OF IM-
PORTANCE:
  2.3.1:   1.   THERE IS A SERICITIC ZONE IN ZONE 1
               (4.834) + +ESTABLISHES 2.3.1 + +

2.3.1:   2. THERE IS A POTASSIC ZONE IN ZONE 2 (4.499)

THERE ARE MANY FACTORS WHICH WOULD HAVE BEEN UN-FAVORABLE HAD NO FAVORABLE FACTOR EXISTED TO OVER-RIDE THEM; IN ORDER OF IMPORTANCE:

2.3.1:   3. THERE IS A BARREN-CORE ZONE IN ZONE 1 (-5.0)

2.3.1:   4. THERE IS A POTASSIC ZONE IN ZONE 1 (-5.0)

2.3.1:   5. THERE IS A PROPYLITIC ZONE IN ZONE 1 (-5.0)

2.3.1:   6. THERE IS A SERICITIC ZONE IN ZONE 2 (-5.0)

2.3.1:   7. THERE IS A POPYLITIC ZONE IN ZONE 2 (-4.989)

2.3.1:   8. THERE IS A BARREN-CORE ZONE IN ZONE 2 (-4.495)

FOR WHICH OF THE ABOVE DO YOU WISH TO SEE ADDI-TIONAL INFORMATION?

- •
- •
- •

Notice the use of the request "Why" in the above consultation; such a command could be given at any time during the consultation. This was important for use in verifying the advice given by PROSPECTOR; otherwise the advice would seem to be generated out of thin air and would not inspire much confidence amongst its users.

Also take note of the marked difference between this conversation and those of Parry or Eliza: rather than trying to establish some sort of rapport, PROSPECTOR is obviously attempting to garner information quickly and efficiently from the user, without recourse to the usual niceties of conversation. Indeed, the user is presumed to be well-schooled in the use of the program, as many of the responses and scores are left unexplained. This is reasonable to some extent in an expert system, as the presumption for many of these systems is that the user would not be consulting the program if he or she were not serious about the material and prepared to devote some time to learning how to use the system. More modern systems often make a greater effort at trying to make a "friendlier" consultation, but the theme remains: the program is simply a powerful tool for expert consultations; any pretenses that it is "smart" are left behind.

MYCIN: COMPUTER MEDICAL ADVICE

Another early expert system was MYCIN, developed in 1976 by Shortliffe. It was a medical expert system designed to diagnose and prescribe medications for bacteriological infections. Like most expert systems, it had the capacity to explain itself, not merely give advice. While this was a useful feature for any expert system, it proved to be critical for MYCIN, as a medical system, and its successors: physicians (and their patients, if any had been prescribed for) were naturally quite anxious to have any computer-generated advice verified by a human, and an explanation of MYCIN's reasoning process was usually central to such verification.

A typical consultation with MYCIN would proceed as recorded below; first the system would make a series of inquiries, and then it would deliver advice (MYCIN's portion of the consultation is capitalized):

WHAT IS THE PATIENT'S NAME?

** John Doe

MALE OR FEMALE?

** Male

AGE?

** He is 55.

HAVE YOU OBTAINED POSITIVE CULTURES INDICATING GENERAL TYPE?

** Yes.

WHAT TYPE OF INFECTION IS IT?

** Primary Bacteremia.

WHEN DID SYMPTOMS FIRST APPEAR?

** May 5.

LET'S CALL THE MOST RECENT POSITIVE CULTURE *CULTURE-1*. FROM WHAT SITE WAS *CULTURE-1* TAKEN?

** From the blood.

WHEN?

** May 9.

LET'S CALL THE FIRST SIGNIFICANT ORGANISM TAKEN FROM THIS CULTURE *ORGANISM-1*. DO YOU KNOW THE IDENTITY OF *ORGANISM-1?*

** No.

IS *ORGANISM-1* A ROD OR A COCCUS OR SOMETHING ELSE?

** Rod.

WHAT IS THE GRAM STAIN OF *ORGANISM-1?*

** Gram-negative.

HAVE THERE BEEN POSITIVE CULTURES FROM SITES THAT ARE NOT ASSOCIATED WITH INFECTIONS ABOUT WHICH YOU ARE SEEKING ADVICE?

** No.

DID *ORGANISM-1* GROW ANAEROBICALLY?

** Yes.

DID *ORGANISM-1* GROW ANAEROBICALLY?

** Yes.

WHAT IS THE SUSPECTED PORTAL OF ENTRY OF *ORGANISM-1?*

** The gastrointestinal tract.

•
•
•

MY RECOMMENDATION WILL BE BASED ON THE OPINION THAT THE IDENTITY OF *ORGANISM-1* MAY BE 1. PSEUDOMONAS-AERUGINOSA 2. KLEBSIELLA-PNEU-

PNEUMONIAE 3. E. COLI 4. BACTEROIDES-FRAGILIS 5. ENTEROBACDTER OR 6. PROTEUS-NON-MIRABILIS.

-
-
-

MY FIRST RECOMMENDATION IS AS FOLLOWS: IN ORDER TO COVER FOR ITEMS 1, 2, 3, 5, AND 6, GIVE GENTAMYCIN USING A DOSE OF 119 MG (1.7 MG/KG) Q8H IV [OR IM] FOR 10 DAYS. MODIFY DOSE IN RENAL FAILURE. AND IN ORDER TO COVER FOR ITEM 4, GIVE CLINDAMYCIN USING A DOSE OF 595 MG (8.5 MG/KG) Q6H IV [OR IM] FOR 14 DAYS. IF DIARRHEA OR OTHER GASTROINTESTINAL SYMPTOMS DEVELOP, CHECK FOR PSEUDOMEMBRANOUS COLITIS.

-
-
-

Eventually, MYCIN gained acceptance as a training tool, as did subsequent generations of medical expert systems; their use as actual treatment tools, however, has yet to gain acceptance other than under the most exceptional circumstances. Most recently, in fact, the U.S. Food and Drug Administration has classified them as requiring FDA approval; the long-term impact of such a move has yet to be fully assessed.

OTHER AREAS OF RESEARCH IN ARTIFICIAL INTELLIGENCE

Using Waltz's 13 categories as a guideline, let us examine the breadth of work in AI and some of its more immediate uses.

Applications and Expert Systems

Applications and expert systems certainly form the broadest category, and one already touched upon. Areas of application beyond that of advice-giving include military applications (guidance, strategy, etc.); rapid retrieval of information from large databases, industrial planning, automation of design and manufacturing processes, text readers for the blind, systems to summarize lengthy texts, fault-finding systems, and more.

Automatic Programming

Automatic programming involves the study of how to allow computers to create programs from the specifications of problems, such as those usually handed to programmers. Beyond reducing the amount of error generated by involving humans in the process, this allows for programs to write specifications for larger, more complex situations in which the size or scope of the problem is beyond the ability for a person or a group of people to accurately represent.

Deduction and Theorem Proving

A more esoteric-appearing area, deduction and theorem proving is the field of study that encompasses the area of automated reasoning. Advances in this field have led to new theorems in mathematics as well as the verification of previously unsolved problems. Less spectacular but nevertheless significant areas of application include the fundamental *heart*, or *inference engine*, of such systems as expert systems, pilot's assistants, and so on.

Knowledge Representation

Knowledge representation is a fundamental area of AI research, whose developments create benefits for virtually every other area of research. The question posed here is how to represent knowledge, whether generated by a computer or extracted from a human. Various techniques and strategies are used, usually balancing gains in speed of retrieval against richness of the knowledge ultimately represented.

Programming Languages and Software

As a highly specialized field, AI has developed its own set of computer languages, which have their own styles, strengths, and weaknesses. One of the oldest of all computer languages, Lisp (for LISt Processing), is the de facto standard for AI development in the U.S. today. Its European counterpart, Prolog (for LOGic PROgramming), has been accepted by the Japanese Fifth Generation project as the foundation for their own AI development language. A less known but extremely powerful language known as Pop-11 (after its developer, Popplestone) is in use almost exclusively in the United Kingdom, but is slowly gaining acceptance elsewhere.

Learning

One of the signs of intelligence is the ability to learn. Thus it should not be surprising that a great deal of research has been devoted to understanding the learning process, and how it might be replicated in machines. While few would say that machines are actually capable of "learning" at this time, many systems could easily pass a pragmatic version of Turing's test when it comes to this area: they modify their own programming based on their interactions with some environment, whether internal or external. Some of the more obvious applications derived from this field of study include systems that read human writing, "understand" human speech, and so on. More subtle applications of gains in this area can be found in virtually every area of AI research.

Natural Language Processing

A number of areas are subsumed under the title of natural language processing, including the ability of machines to accept human language, whether written or spoken, as input computer-generated speech, known as *speech synthesis*; and language understanding, as distinct from speech synthesis, in that some "understanding" of the words expressed in natural langauge is strived for.

Problem Solving, Control Methods, and Searching

Problem solving, control methods and search are areas that are at the same time distinct and yet overlapping. In solving problems, whether they be real-world problems or "toy" problems, such as the classic missionary and savages problem or the fifteen-square puzzle, a great deal of thought must be given to how one will search the potential solutions for the correct one, as well as how one develops and implements the control strategies needed in such programs.

Robotics

A field often considered distinct from AI in recent times, robotics was probably first grouped with AI simply because of the science fiction quality of its subject matter. Nowadays, industrial robots are becoming commonplace and discussions about them have expanded quite naturally to include mechanical and electrical engineering, among other topics. In this book the AI issues generic to robotics will be treated as part and parcel of more traditional AI topics (control strategies, pattern recognition, and so on), and robotics will not be treated separately.

Vision

How to get visual information in a form computers can use has been a serious issue for many years. Now the problem has evolved from the search for simple representation methods through the issues of recognition of shapes and objects to a field called *scene analysis*, which involves getting a computer to make some contextual statement about "what is going on" in a scene, rather than simply identify the objects in it.

Cognitive Modeling and Psychological Studies of Intelligence

As computer scientists realized that much of the work of understanding the reasoning process had been started by psychologists many years before, they quickly moved to incorporate that work into the body of AI research. Efforts in this area have impact for knowledge representation schemes, algorithms for AI, and computer-aided instruction.

Specialized AI Architectures

Some of the issues raised by the development of AI systems are so resource-intensive that hardware architectures have been developed in an attempt to meet these requirements. Two companies in the United States, Symbolics and Lisp Machines, Inc., were founded simply to provide computers that are devoted to high-speed LISP language processing. Other major corporations like Xerox, Hewlett-Packard, Digital Equipment Corp, and Texas Instruments have released so-called *AI workstations*—special-purpose computers for AI research.

Social and Philosophical Issues

Naturally, research as far reaching as that proposed by AI could not be undertaken without raising fundamental philosophic issues; additionally, as the major source of funding has become military in nature, numerous social issues have arisen.

SUMMARY

Artificial intelligence has its origins in science fiction stories about human-like machines. Its applications are increasing in number in everyday life. From the first efforts to pass off programs as people to current efforts to deliver the knowledge and wisdom of human experts, efforts in this area have taken scientists into studies of vision, thought, psychology, and philosophy. Now this research is beginning to bear fruit, and it will be to the informed person that the first benefits fall. It is no longer necessary, however, to understand the full expanse of research to make informed decisions about the use of AI technology in everyday life; indeed, such an endeavor is well beyond the capabilities of any one person to achieve. Nonetheless, this book contains a survey of the terrain sufficient to enable the ambitious business manager to begin to make use of this exciting, challenging, and ever-changing field.

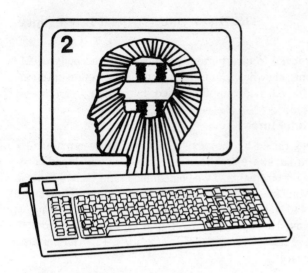

Theoretical Foundations

During the process of trying to make computer programs that exhibit artificial intelligence, some fundamental questions must be answered—often, admittedly on a purely pragmatic basis. For example, a concern central to most AI programs is, How will knowledge be represented in this system? Other standard questions that must be answered are, How will knowledge be retrieved from this system? In what manner will the user communicate with the program? What strategies will be used in arriving at answers to the problem posed by the user? and so on.

These questions strike at the core of philosophy and psychology, and as such represent the original drive to explore artificial intelligence. Taking the above questions as examples, notice the fundamental issues that are raised:

"How will knowledge be represented in this system?" At issue here is the structure (and hence the definition) of knowledge. When we say that someone "knows" something, what does that mean? If it is said, for example, that Jane knows about restaurants, what is it that she has? Is it simply a list of facts about restaurants, in no particular order? If the ordering is important, what order is necessary? Or best? If an ordered list is an insufficient description, what else is needed—perhaps some connections between the facts? For example, might it be said that "Wine is a kind of drink," or will it be necessary to say that "Wine is a kind of alcoholic beverage; Alcoholic beverages may only be consumed by sober patrons over the legal drinking age?" Are there different "levels" of facts, such as "Wine is more expensive than soda" versus "House white wine is $2.00 per glass" and "Soda water is $1.50?" What about rules and procedures, like "You must pay before you leave?" Do you need specific rules for every restaurant, such as for prices, or can some form of a menu be used? Taking this even further, is all of one's knowledge about restaurants specific to restaurants, or is some of it generalized from knowledge about more general things, like stores and eating? If so, how do you decide which portions of common sense need representation, and which do not? Will anything be lost in the process of representing that portion of common sense that is applicable to restaurants that would somehow "damage" the set of common sense knowledge by its absence?

It is easy to see how quickly things become complicated when one is trying to represent knowledge (as opposed to simple data) in a computer. This level of complexity is reached so quickly, in fact, that the problem of knowledge representation is one of the central issues to be addressed in AI, both for philosophic and pragmatic reasons.

The question of knowledge retrieval is not only similar to that of knowledge representation, but it is actually intimately linked to it. How one chooses to represent knowledge in the computer will have a direct impact on how one retrieves it, and strategies for one will influence strategies for the other. Notice for instance, the difference between storing an unordered list of facts and an ordered list: clearly, different strategies will have to be used in order to achieve the most efficient knowledge retrieval possible.

Similarly, if one has decided that there will be hierarchies of rules, how does one search for the relevant sub-rule? If we want to retrieve the relevant knowledge about wine, how will this be accomplished? How far up the hierarchy will we need to go? For example, will saying "Wine is a kind of beverage" be sufficient, or will we need to specify that it is alcoholic? Will we need to say what is done with beverages, or will that be too involved? And what will be the most efficient manner of retrieving that knowledge?

The combination of knowledge representation and knowledge retrieval, therefore, presents one of the greatest, if not *the* greatest, challenge to AI programming at present. The need to store large amounts of data ("knowledge") and retrieve it quickly has led to new hardware technologies for storage and new algorithms (or strategies) for retrieval. The Japanese effort at bringing AI to their computing systems has, in fact, focused on this problem as the central issue: they have devoted the lion's share of their fiscal and personnel resources to the development of new hardware and computer languages for the processing and management of large amounts of data.

The issue of communication with the user raises fundamental questions about the nature of communication in addition to questions concerning the specifics of how to manage input and output. How much of a natural language will be used by the computer for output, and how much will be accepted as input? How will the gaps in this language that must ultimately arise be handled? What sort of gaps and how many of them can be allowed if the sense of natural language is to be retained?

What is it that enhances communication between the computer and the user? Is it acceptable to use only input from a typewriter-like keyboard, or should other mediums and strategies be utilized? When is a *mouse* helpful, and when not? Digitizing tablets? Light pens? Spoken input? And as for output, when should graphics be used? Computer-generated speech? Video displays from laser disks? Manipulation of physical objects? Do these input and output features enhance the communication or restrict it? Under what circumstances?

Another central issue is that of the strategies used for processing the knowledge. Here we raise issues generic to the question of reasoning itself. Is simple logic sufficient? Do people *really* reason logically, in the classic sense, or does their use of intuition constitute another kind of logic? If so, do we want computers to be intuitive, or is that actually a disadvantage? If we want some alternative reasoning styles, how will we express the rules for them? And how much of these styles are dependent upon the specific knowledge present? Some? A little? A great deal?

Developing the *inference engine*, as it is referred to in the field, is one of the most subtle efforts an AI developer can make: this sets the stage for how all decisions will be made, and minor variations can have far-reaching consequences that may or may not be immediately obvious in the final system. In this chapter we will explore three of the classic alternatives, as well as look briefly at some of the more application-specific options. We shall approach, in turn, classic logic, Bayesian inference, and fuzzy logic.

Traditionally, the logical structure used in computers (as well as in philosophy) was that of classic, or Aristotelean, logic. Most people are familiar with elements of classic logic, but owing to its centrality to the field of AI, it is worth reviewing here.

In classic logic, there are nine rules of inference, along with three so-called "laws of thought." Together, these make up the procedures that are usually included, in some form or another, in every computer system—not only in AI systems. Before exploring these rules and laws, however, some terminology must be established. In logic, we speak of *propositions*, which may be either true or false. Examples of propositions are:

> Rover is a dog.
> The sky is green.
> It is raining outside.

Propositions can be grouped together to form an *argument*, such as:

> All dogs have fleas.
> Rover is a dog.

Therefore,

Rover has fleas.

This argument is made up of three propositions, the first two of which are *premises*, and the last of which is the *conclusion*. Every argument has at least one premise, and has exactly one conclusion. Along the way, interim conclusions may be drawn from sets of premises and then used as premises for a later conclusion. For example:

Water is a clear liquid.
If I am ill, then I should drink clear liquids.

Therefore,

If I am ill, then I should drink water.

I am ill.

Therefore,

I should drink water.

The process of determining the truth or falsity of a conclusion from its premises is known as *inferencing*; this is the basis for the name given to the set of procedures for managing this process in computers—the *inference engine*.

The most commonly known rule of inference is that of *Modus Ponens*. It has the general form:

$$\frac{\begin{array}{l} p > q \\ p \end{array}}{q}$$

In English, an example would be:

If it is raining, then I am wet.
It is raining.

Therefore,

I am wet.

In this case, the statement "It is raining" corresponds to the variable p, and "I am wet" with q. The symbolic notation p > q is formally read as "p implies q," or more commonly, "If p, then q."

The other common rule is that of *Modus Tollens*:

$$\frac{\begin{array}{l} p > g \\ \sim q \end{array}}{\sim p}$$

The ~ sign means *not*. Thus, using the above example, the English version would be:

If it is raining, then I am wet.
I am not wet.

Therefore,

It is not raining.

Now, certainly there are ways of imagining how I could be not wet and it could be raining: I might be indoors or under an umbrella. The point here is that I can draw the conclusion "It is not raining" from the premises without fear, given the rule of Modus Tollens.

Two other symbols are important in classic logic. They are used to join two or more propositions into a single proposition: ^ (for AND) and ^ (for OR). Rules of inference making use of each of these are, first, Simplification:

$$\frac{p \ {}^{\wedge} \ q}{p}$$

It is raining AND I am wet.

Therefore,

I am wet.

and secondly, Addition:

$$\frac{p}{p \lor q}$$

It is raining.

Therefore,

It is raining OR I am wet.

These are trivial examples, but they provide the building blocks of logical inference. Other rules of inference are more involved. Let us presume that:

> r = I will get sick.
> s = It is cold.
> t = I will stay home.

One rule of inference is that of Hypothetical Syllogism:

$$\frac{\begin{array}{l} p > q \\ q > r \end{array}}{p > r}$$

If it is raining, then I am wet.
If I am wet, then I will get sick.

Therefore,

If it is raining, then I will get sick.

Another is Constructive Dilemma:

$$\frac{\begin{array}{l} (p > q) \wedge (s > t) \\ p \wedge r \end{array}}{q \wedge t}$$

It is true that

If it is raining, then I am wet.

AND

If it is cold, then I will stay home.
It is either raining or cold.

Therefore,

Either I am wet, or I will stay home.

The remaining rules can be found at the end of the chapter; for now, the above are sufficient to convey the sense of logical propositions and rules of inference.

Also important to logic, and as we will see, to fuzzy logic, are the so-called *Laws of Thought*. Briefly, these can be stated as:

The Law of Identity: 'A' is 'A'; or, "A dog is a dog."

The Law of Contradiction: 'A' is not 'not-A'; or, "A full jar is not empty."

The Law of the Excluded Middle: Everything is 'A' or 'not-A'; or, "The light is on or it is off."

It is this final law, the Law of the Excluded Middle, which is most subject to debate, and which gives rise to fuzzy logic, which we will address shortly.

The applications to standard computer programming in most cases are straightforward. For example, the Law of the Excluded Middle can be translated into the digital, binary representation of everything in a computer: everything is on (1) or off (0). Likewise, *Modus Ponens* is the typical If/Then structure. As in BASIC:

```
100  IF RAINING = 1 THEN WET = 1
```

Even the Hypothetical Syllogism is easy:

```
100  IF RAINING = 1 THEN WET = 1
110  IF WET = 1 THEN SICK = 1
```

The constructive dilemma, however, is not easily represented, since in the computer, a state must either be true or not true; it is not easy to represent the fact that one of two variables is equal to one, but not state explicitly which one it is.

The theme here is that traditional computer programming is not merely similar to classic logic; it is in fact founded upon it and entirely dependent upon it. Thus we have assumed an inference engine from the beginning, if we do not make any efforts to modify or enhance classic logic. And it can be shown that classic logic is inadequate for representing the full scope of human reasoning. Let us examine fuzzy logic as the first case in point:

You will recall that the Law of the Excluded Middle states that everything must either be true or false; there is no room for any values in between (the Excluded Middle). Thus, the light is either on, or it is off. It is either raining, or it is not . . . and so on.

While this may be true in a formal sense, however, people often view the world less crisply, in a more "fuzzy" manner. For example, if it were misting outside, and you were asked, "Is it raining outside?" you would be hard pressed to answer yes or no. Instead, you would likely answer something like "sort of," or "not really," by which you would mean some intermediate answer, something between yes and no.

This is characteristic of the way people reason. While it may be possible to use a series of questions that *could* be answered yes or no to replace the question "Is it raining outside?" such a series would most certainly lose the spirit of the single, simple question and answer. For example, the interchange might proceed like this:

> Is is Raining?
> > No.
> Is it Dry?
> > No.
> Is it Sprinkling?
> > No.
> Is it Misting?
> > Yes.

And so on.

Now, Heraclitus (999 B.C.) was the first to "publicize" the Law of the Excluded Middle, and he had opposition from the start. Since that time, a number of philosophers and mathematicians have attempted to devise alternatives, all in the hopes of allowing everyday language to be represented more effectively in logic. One idea, in various incarnations, was to try and create a single middle value, having the meaning *possibly*, or something similar. But with each suggestion, a series of mathematical hoops had to be gone through: logic is the foundation of mathematics, and any new logic that was proposed had to be able to generate the same sort of mathematics that everyone was used to; otherwise its utility would be limited. And none of the proposed alternative (multivalued) logics were successful in this way.

In the early sixties, though, an engineer by the name of Lotfi Zadeh proposed a new approach, which he called *fuzzy systems*, as a manner of representing intermediate values between true and false. Here is how it worked.

In order to generate standard mathematics, mathematicians would assign the value of 0 to false and 1 to true, and then use a set of conventions for translating logical propositions into mathematical equations. The idea was that the operation OR was converted to addition, and AND was converted to multiplication. Finally, in order to make certain that you only received a 1 or a 0 as a result, any time the answer was greater than 1, it remained 1. For example:

> If A is true and B is false, what is the truth of the statement, A and B are true?

This translates into:

> A = 1
> B = 0

A * B = ?

The answer is 0, so the statement "A and B are true" is false. Now, while that may seem simple to determine, there are two benefits to this sort of an exercise. As mentioned previously, using this sort of a method allows the whole of mathematics to be derived from Logic, which makes for a nice, orderly world, from a philosopher's or a mathematician's, point of view. On the more immediately practical side, however, there is an interest in being able to take complicated arguments and generate some indication of their truth or falsehood. Often the propositions contained in these arguments will be long and involved, and there will be many of them. Having a method of automatically processing them is one way of not only saving time, but of being certain that your results are accurate. So, no one is particularly interested in "trying out" a new mathematics!

Previously, attempts at multivalued logic added one or more values to the range of true or false, such as the range [0, 1, 2] (Lukasiewicz); or [–1, 0, +1] (Knuth); or [0, 1, 2, 3] (Lukasiewicz again). But all of these yielded mathematics that were difficult to use, and/or were counterintuitive.

Zadeh's insight was to allow for an *infinite* range of values between 0 and 1, and to suggest two slightly different operations to take the place of addition and multiplication. In place of addition (OR), he used the MAX function, or maximum. Thus, when comparing two values for the OR function, take the larger of the two (written MAX [A, B]). Likewise, instead of using multiplication (AND), he used MIN (for minimum), written MIN [A, B]. Now if one compares the results generated (in classic logic) with these functions to those generated through addition and multiplication, it is discovered that the results are identical. For example:

True AND False:
$$1 * 0 = 0$$
$$MIN [1, 0] = 0$$

True OR False:
$$1 + 0 = 1$$
$$MAX [1, 0] = 1$$

False AND False:
$$0 * 0 = 0$$
$$MIN [0, 0] = 0$$

True OR True:
$$1 + 1 = 2, \text{ must be converted to } 1$$
$$MAX [1, 1] = 1$$

As is quickly seen, even the untidiness of the use of addition for OR is taken care of. Now, when it comes to fuzzy values, how are they used? Let us use the following statements for an example: Let us assign the statement "Jane is tall" to A, and "Jane is smart" to B. Furthermore, let us assume that Jane is very tall, or A = 0.9, and she is very smart, or B = 0.9. Now, notice that the assignment of 0.9 to represent the degree "very" is completely arbitrary; fuzzy logic in and of itself makes no effort to tell us what values we should assign to what natural language terms. Instead, fuzzy logic gives us a *vehicle* for processing these values once we have translated them from English to mathematics.

Here is what happens to the fuzzy logic statements:

A AND B:

Jane is tall and Jane is smart.

0.9 * 0.9 = 0.81
MIN [0.9, 0.9] = 0.9

A OR B:

Jane is tall or Jane is smart.

0.9 + 0.9 = 1.8, converted to 1
MAX [0.9, 0.9] = 0.9

In the first case, *A AND B*, notice that multiplication produces a lower result than that of the MIN function. Thus, Jane is less of a smart, tall person than she is a tall person and a smart person. Rendered into English, if 0.9 is "very" and 0.81 (being less) is "quite," then the classic version reads:

If Jane is very tall, and Jane is very smart, then she is a quite tall, smart person.

whereas fuzzy logic would result in:

If Jane is very tall, and Jane is very smart, then she is a very tall, smart person.

The proponents of fuzzy logic maintain that the second statement is a closer representation of the way people think and speak than is the first. More importantly, realize that a series of "very" values (or any value less than 1) will ultimately reduce the value of the final statement to something approaching 0, or false, in classic logic. Thus, saying that Jane was very smart, very tall, very fast, very thoughtful, very talkative, and very happy would yield a statement like "Jane is sort of smart, tall, fast, thoughtful, talkative, and happy"—clearly not what most people would expect.

The opposite results take place when replacing addition with the MAX function: whereas addition tends to keep increasing values, MAX leaves them stable, thus preventing a string of nearly false values from generating a nearly true result.

The critical benefit of fuzzy logic is that it leaves mathematics essentially intact; thus, it can be substituted for classic logic, with its binary (2) truth values, giving instead literally an infinity of values with which to express the subtleties of human language and reasoning.

SUMMARY

Artificial intelligence is a field that cuts across a number of disciplines, offering each a challenge. To the philosopher, it grants the opportunity to explore the nature of learning, of intelligent life, and of meaning. To the linguist, it offers the chance to explore new types of language and new ways of understanding natural languages. To the mathematician, it offers new applications for statistics, theorem proving, and logic. To the psychologist, it offers the opportunity to explore the nature of understanding and communication. To the physiologist, artificial intelligence provides the chance to explore the functioning of the sensory organs, the skeletal system, the musculature, and more. And, finally, to the computer scientist, artificial intelligence offers the challenge to yet again create something new for the benefit of humanity.

Knowledge Representation Schemes

The central problem in artificial intelligence is the management of large amounts of information, whether as a function of storage, retrieval, or processing. In the attempt to build computer systems that are capable of functioning more like humans, the question immediately becomes one of trying to make the quantities of information that a person has available to the computer. The reason for this is that having large volumes of information available is a prerequisite for many abilities: to handle incompletely understood situations, for example, it is important to have a rich body of information from which to draw so that similarities may be searched for and inferences drawn. Another important requisite is that this information must be readily accessible, for purposes of comparison as well as for quick switching from one topic to another.

There are many forms that knowledge can take, as the average person understands the term *knowledge*. First of all, there is the straightforward collection of facts that we all possess to one degree or another; as an example, the fact "The sky is blue" is in most of our stores of knowledge. Someone who has exceptional abilities in this form of knowledge representation, we might surmise, would be an excellent contestant at games of trivia. This form of knowledge, however, must be distinguished from the simple list of facts that makes up a dictionary or encyclopedia: knowledge resides in the ability to use information, not just store it.

A second, slightly more abstract form of knowledge representation might be called knowledge about events, or interactions between knowledge items from the first category, usually embedded with a sense of time. Typical knowledge items in this group are "The dog barked at the cat," and "I ate scrod for dinner last night."

The next, more abstract form of knowledge is that of procedural knowledge: how one does things or accomplishes certain tasks. Knowledge items of this type can be thought of as rules to be used under certain conditions; this implies a greater interaction with the world. In order to know which rule to apply, we must complete an assessment of the situation at hand. Thus, we might have knowledge at this level expressed as the following: "If you are hungry, eat dinner," or "If it is raining and you plan to go outside, wear a raincoat or take an umbrella, unless it is a mild shower, it is summer, and you are planning to swim in the immediate future."

Finally, the most abstract form of knowledge might be called *metaknowledge*, or knowing about knowing. Examples of this form of knowledge are somewhat more difficult to describe, but could be thought of as strategies for problem solving. A low-level metarule would be knowing that the four central squares on a chessboard are usually powerful points to occupy in a game of chess, as opposed to the less abstract form of knowledge that a bishop only moves in a diagonal direction. A higher level of abstraction would be the ability to create a game that is similar in spirit to chess, but with different rules.

All of these forms of knowledge have significance when it comes to the question of how knowledge is acquired, stored, processed, and added to. It will be necessary, after all, for an "intelligent" computer not only to be able to perform in a manner that appears intelligent but to actually benefit from its experience. Thus, any information that is stored in the computer must be easily accessed, easily built upon, and capable of being processed both quickly and in a manner that produces "intelligent" results. Furthermore, since all software systems need to be maintained and updated by people, this *knowledge base* (as the repository of knowledge is referred to) must be organized in a fashion that is at least accessible to people, and preferably congruent with the way that people think. Obviously, these requirements pose no small problem to the designers of programs that make use of artificial intelligence.

As an example of human intellectual functioning and its relevance to knowledge representation, let us take the case of recognizing familiar faces in a crowd. Every one of us—with certain bizarre exceptions that, significantly, appear to be rooted in physical brain disorders—has the capability to recognize people that we know out of a set of unfamiliar faces. While people possess this power to varying degrees, it is an ability that is perhaps one of the first tasks for infants to master, and that can take on many forms: the person who has problems remembering names but "never forgets a face," or the savant who appears to have an inexhaustible library of names and faces, all quickly retrievable.

Many questions arise about this ability that serve to highlight the problems faced in the field of artificial intelligence. One is the question of storage: how are these facial images stored? If we consider the problem of amounts of storage required, we are faced with a staggering statistic: the amount of storage required at first appears to be beyond the physical capacity of the brain: If we presume (naively) that visual images are stored in the same manner as television pictures or newspaper prints, then we can calculate the number of *pixels*, or picture elements, required for a sufficiently detailed image to be stored.

A computer monitor, used for what is considered medium-resolution graphics display, can display 600 × 240 dots, or pixels, each of which can assume one of 16 colors. It takes 4 bits to store a number between 1 and 16, or 1/2 byte. Thus, an image of the resolution mentioned would require 72,000 bytes, or about 70 kilobytes. This style of image representation is known as *bit-mapping*.

Bit mapping corresponds to the lowest level of abstraction mentioned above: faces are merely objects, taken out of context, out of any relationship with their surroundings. It might be correctly argued that this is not the way that people *usually* think, and we will address alternative methods later. For now, however, let us proceed with this approach, since it is within human capability to recognize a face *without* a particularly rich context.

As mentioned above, a bit-mapped image of medium resolution would require approximately 70K of storage. (This number is probably too small, as we have the ability to remember details of images that are much more detailed (highly resolved) than that; however, we shall proceed with this conservative figure for now.) If one estimates the number of faces the average person can recognize, including friends, neighbors, coworkers, famous people, and so on, a thousand appears to be a reasonable number. This means that the storage requirements *simply for faces* would be on the order of 70,000K, or 70 million bytes! And remember, all of that information must be available rapidly: recall how quickly people recognize faces in a crowd!

It would be nice, therefore, if it were not necessary to store all information in the form of bit-maps, as this can be a particularly "expensive" type of storage, in terms of the volume required. Turning to the field of computer science for ideas, there is another storage strategy that may be useful. By attempting to reduce the amount of redundant data through the use of special codes, we can reduce the total amount of storage resources required. And, if the data to be stored is particularly well-suited to the method chosen, a tremendous amount of storage can be conserved.

One coding method within this set of strategies is that of preceding every data item with a number, indicating how many repetitions there are of that datum. Taking the statistics above, let us presume that there are 16 colors available for our picture, labeled A through P. If A corresponds to black (or some background color), then a picture of a square might appear in a bit-mapped representation as follows:

```
A   A   A   A   A   A   A   A

A   A   A   A   A   A   A   A

A   A   B   B   B   B   A   A

A   A   B   C   C   B   A   A

A   A   B   C   C   B   A   A

A   A   B   B   B   B   A   A

A   A   A   A   A   A   A   A

A   A   A   A   A   A   A   A
```

In the above example, the square is made up of Bs, with an interior of 4 Cs, and a border, two-deep, of As around it. The coding method described above would yield the following representation:

```
8A
8A
2A4B2A
2A1B2C1B2A
2A1B2C1B2A
2A4B2A
8A
8A
```

The result of this system is that 40 characters are used to encode the data, rather than the 64 originally used. While this represents a significant savings, however, it is not difficult to imagine a set of circumstances under which this strategy can backfire, and actually result in a loss of storage: notice that each letter must be preceded by at least one number; thus for data that do not repeat, there is a net *loss* of one character. Therefore, if a picture contained a sufficiently large number of single data items, there could actually be a loss of storage efficiency.

A further problem arises when the overall efficiency of the system is considered. There is not actually a *gain* in savings until there are three characters found in a row. Now, this (or any other) coding strategy is going to put an additional drain on the processing requirements of the system, since the images must be encoded as they are received and decoded before they can be processed. Thus, the amount of redundancy of particular data items must be substantial if there is to be a final usefulness in a system that is operating in real time, as people do.

A final observation, however, is the most crucial: while the above strategy (and similar ones) point the way to more efficient data storage, they do not represent any shift in the conceptual model used to represent images: they are still functioning with the model of bit mapping, and thus they inherit all the problems of such an approach. Since one of the goals of artificial intelligence is to make computers that function in a manner similar to that of humans (when such an approach is warranted), an entirely different representation scheme would appear to be in order.

When someone is asked to describe another person, they will most often give a list of that person's features, along with some description of those features. For example, I might say that Ted has a thick beard, bright red hair, and a large mouth. The notion embodied here is that faces consist of a variety of structures: eyes, ears, nose, mouth, hair, and so on, and that each of these features can be characterized in a meaningful manner. Thus, Ted's representation might be described as the following: hair (red, short, wiry); beard (present); mouth (wide) and so on. This would dramatically reduce the amount of storage required, and in fact it corresponds to the manner in which people tend to verbally describe each other.

Such an approach could be imagined to operate by having a list of the standard facial structures, each of which would be associated with a particular description of that feature. So long as these descriptions were coded in some abstract manner, this strategy would both save on storage and come closer to the way that people describe, at least at an abstract level, each other.

Another component of this approach is what might be labeled *exception reporting* in traditional data processing: the process of listing only those features that are different enough to warrant mention (in other words, are *descriptive* of the individual). Again, by not mentioning those features that are normal or ordinary, a great deal of storage can be conserved.

Yet, it is not as though we do not remember these ordinary features of people's faces; we can usually give a complete description of someone's appearance if necessary; we just don't reference these features initially when we are trying to identify or describe someone. Thus, perhaps it is the case that these subsequent descriptions reside in some form of "secondary storage," only to be retrieved when required.

While such a storage scheme *does* parallel certain descriptive techniques used by people, and it *does* conserve on storage, it does not fully capture the manner in which we describe our images of others. No matter how good or bad an artist or individual may be at recognizing people, every one of us is capable of calling up complete images of people that we know (as in daydreams). This image in principle would seem to be of sufficient detail as to correspond to a bit-mapping scheme; we therefore seem to be left with the notion that we utilize *both* approaches, resulting in perhaps a greater efficiency where processing is concerned, but an overall loss in terms of storage space. And yet, even further complications can be explored.

It is not only the case that this information must be readily available for recall, but it must be able to be accessed in a manner that makes rapid comparisons possible. Again, consider the fact that, as far as our mental experience is concerned, we don't run through a list of 1,000 faces every time we see a face to determine (a) if we know them or not, and (b) who they are; instead, the question of whether we know them or not seems to be immediately available, and the question of who they are is often resolved by searching associative information: where we seem to recognize them from, and so on. As if that weren't complication enough, we also have the ability to recognize facial structures and associate them with the quality of being related in the biological sense: it is easy for someone to say, usually with a great deal of accuracy, "Oh, you must be Jane's sister!" In all probability such a statement could be made by someone who had never seen a picture of Jane's sister before.

Also consider the party game of recognizing people from their pictures as children: this requires a knowledge (albeit intuitive) as to how people's features change over time; of facial structures that remain consistent over time; of how to relate someone's current context with prior contexts; in short, it requires a tremendous body of "common sense" knowledge about appearances, as well as the ability to draw conclusions from very poorly specified data.

Each of these examples indicates that there is a tremendous amount of cross referencing (and/or indexing) that takes place in our "computerized" view of the human brain, which again would tend to speed up the processing times but put even further demands on storage resources. So our attempt at studying the brain as a method of making our use of storage more efficient appears in the short run to have backfired; instead, we have found ourselves needing more space than originally intended, albeit with the ultimate advantage of increasing our processing speed and accuracy.

While the specifics of how the brain actually stores and retrieves information are only dimly known at present, and as such have little direct application to storage strategies in computers, we can nonetheless attempt to create methods of storage, processing, and retrieval that correspond to these ideas.

The lowest level of knowledge representation is typified by the approach taken in the Prolog language: facts, rules, and operations are collected, and the language manages to draw conclusions when queried from this knowledge base, without requiring the user to know a lot about exactly *how* the conclusions are being reached. The Prolog language is discussed in more depth in another chapter; for now, it will be sufficient to simply examine the knowledge base for a classic set of knowledge: information regarding membership in a family tree.

In what is perhaps the most cryptic portion of the following example, Prolog first requires that a number of operators be declared. In the case of a family tree, these operators could be:

```
:- op(200, yf,   is_male).
:- op(200, yf,   is_female).
:- op(200, xfx,  is_a_parent_of).
:- op(200, xfx,  is_a_child_of).
:- op(200, xfx,  is_the_mother_of).
:- op(200, xfx,  is_the_father_of).
:- op(200, xfx,  is_a_sibling_of).
:- op(200, xfx,  married).
:- op(200, xfx,  is_married_to).
```

and so on.

Next, it is necessary to establish the facts for the family tree: who is married to whom, who has children, what their names are, and so on. While some of these facts may appear trivial, remember that the knowledge base, in order to be useful, will have to be as complete, rich, and consistent as possible.

```
stella is_female.
ed is_male.
stella married ed.

warren is_a_child_of stella.
warren is_a_child_of ed.
warren is_male.

john is_a_child_of stella.
john is_a_child_of ed.
john is_male.
sally is_female.
john married sally.

mark is_a_child_of sally.
mark is_a_child_of john.
mark is_male.
fran is_female.
mark married fran.
```

Artificial Intelligence: Theory, Logic and Application

The next step is to present the particular rules, or procedures for how to infer information from the collection of facts and operators. The first rule is trivial: someone, let's say X, is married to someone else, let's say Y, if X married Y or if Y married X; in other words, the order of names in the "married" phrase has no bearing on the two people being married: they are both married to each other. In Prolog, the rule looks like this:

```
X is_married_to Y :-    X married Y;
                        Y married X.
```

The symbol ":-" means IF, ";" means OR, and "," means AND. Thus, the rule for fathers would be written:

```
X is_the_father_of Y :- X is_a_parent_of Y,
                        X is_male.
```

A more complicated rule is that for establishing one's siblings:

```
X is_a_sibling_of Y   :- A is_the_mother_of X,
                         A is_the_mother_of Y,
                         B is_the_father_of X,
                         B is_the_father_of Y,
                         X \= Y.
```

This rule states that if X and Y have the same mother and father, *and* they are not the same person (X $\setminus$ = Y means X is not equal to Y), then they are siblings.

Further examples of Prolog can be found in the chapter on languages for artificial intelligence.

In traditional computing, data is stored in one of two fashions: either as "raw" data or "records." In "raw" format, in data is stored sequentially, without any particular regard to the actual information it represents. This approach is only used under circumstances where the data is relatively homogenous, such as the data for a bit-mapped image. This type of storage technique, while occasionally more efficient in terms of the space used, makes retrieval of specific portions of that data difficult and slow.

The more common approach to data storage is to organize it into blocks that "make sense," or convey *as part of their actual architecture* some representation of the structure of the information that was their source. Thus, an employee record might have these blocks, or *fields*: NAME. AD-DRESS, SOCIAL_SECURITY_NUMBER, and DATE_OF_BIRTH. Taking this route has two advantages: first, it allows for faster retrieval of specific items (since one can retrieve a specific field, or at worst a specific record); and second, it more closely resembles the manner in which we think about things, and thus is easier for analysts, programmers, and other computer staff to manage. Needless to say, no benefit comes without cost, and it is usually the case that such a method will result in greater storage requirements.

The similarity between records and the second method of representing faces should now be clear. In the field of artificial intelligence, designers have taken this concept one step further, under the initial guidance of Marvin Minsky, and developed the concept of *frames*. Frames are another, highly similar strategy for representing knowledge, that at a first glance is indistinguishable from records. In fact, at a sufficiently deep level, they are *quite* similar to records, but it is the intermediate range that proves to be the most interesting.

In records, individual units of information are organized into *fields*; in frames, these are known as *slots*. For the most part, these slots function in manner identical to fields: they identify a particular *type* of information through their own labeling and contain the specifics for that particular knowledge object.

Frames are organized into networks, propagating downward, when needed, from the most general instances of an object type (or class) to specific examples of that class. For example, a generic frame about faces might be represented as follows:

```
Generic FACE Frame
      Specialization_of:    BODY_PARTS
      Number_of_eyes:       integer (DEFAULT = 2)
      Color_of_eyes:        blue, brown, hazel, ...
      Number_of_ears:       integer (DEFAULT = 2)
      Color_of_hair:        brown, red, white, ...
```

etc.

Ted's face would be represented by another frame, such as:

```
TEDS_FACE Frame
      Specialization_of:    FACE
      Number_of_eyes:       2
      Color_of_eyes:        brown
      Number_of_ears:       2
      Color_of_hair:        red
```

etc.

Inherent in each frame is the notion of "ancestry," namely that the

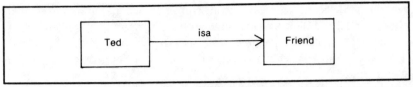

Fig. 3-1. The beginning of a semantic network representing knowledge about a person.

Frame TEDS__FACE has some sort of code that allows it to be traced directly back to the FACE frame. Likewise, there could be frames "beneath" TEDS__FACE, as well as frames above FACE.

This approach, while it almost certainly does not directly describe the manner in which knowledge is encoded in the brain, does represent a more "human" style of expression: like people do, it breaks information up into modularized units that can be called upon as necessary. As such, it represents a richer version of the lowest level of knowledge representation.

Another approach for representing knowledge is the notion of *semantic networks*. While there is some similarity between frames and semantic networks, there is a different flavor to the manner in which they represent knowledge, and therefore they will be found more useful by some people, and less by others.

A typical network to express knowledge about Ted might begin as shown in Fig. 3-1.

Abstracting further, we might note that all our friends are people (e.g., not dogs). The resulting network is shown in Fig. 3-2. We link TED and

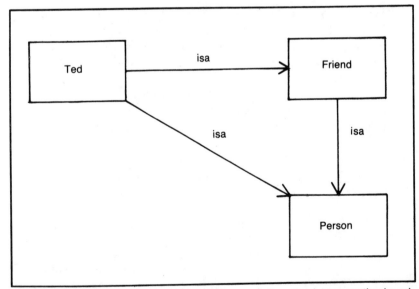

Fig. 3-2. A second step in the development of a semantic network representing knowledge about a person.

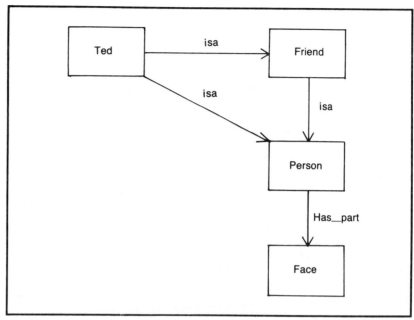

Fig. 3-3. Further development of a semantic network representing knowledge about a person.

PERSON because TED is a PERSON irrespective of whether or not he is a friend. Next, it can be said that all people have faces; thus the resulting network is shown in Fig. 3-3.

This network can become more and more complex as concepts and relationships are added: the notion of ownership, time, and so on can be represented simply by creating boxes and labeling arrows. As the knowledge representation scheme becomes richer, however, the complexity grows as well, and the resources required to store, retrieve, and otherwise manage the knowledge base grows even more quickly.

It will be noticed that the semantic network, while providing a richness that is not so easily (or perhaps graphically) achieved with frames, nonetheless lacks the ability for executing steps in a sequence. Thus, rules, procedures, and so on are not easily expressed in this form. In order to accomplish the next phase of abstraction, another approach must be utilized. One likely candidate for this requirement is the concept of scripts, as devised by Dr. Terry Winograd.

Scripts have the general appearance of frames, except that they contain directives for actions to be taken, which may in fact be only conditionally executed, and they convey a sense of sequence as well. As such, they resemble a computer program, but at a much higher level of abstraction. As an example, Dr. Winograd developed a script for actions to be taken in a restaurant, which might have appeared something like this:

```
EVENT_SEQUENCE:
    first:    go_in_the_door Script
    then:     if (wait_for_seating_sign OR reservations)
                 then wait Script
    then:     sit_down Script
    then:     review_menu Script
    then:     if (food_acceptable)
                 then order Script
    then:     eat Script
    then:     pay Script
    finally:  leave_restaurant Script
```

Each of the scripts mentioned above would be a series of sequences like the above, and each would be called upon in its turn when required by the script "above" it. Scripts can be nested to any degree desired; as a result, their management by the computer can be quite involved as one "gets deep into" the script.

Ultimately, all these methods of knowledge representation are recorded as series of 0s and 1s, the same as other, more mundane data is stored in computers every day. One approach may have some apparent benefits for a particular application over another approach, but those differences and advantages are only recognized by the people interacting with the computer: for the machinery itself, it makes no difference whatsoever. It is thus the person that is the final arbiter of what makes sense and what does not—whether from the designer's point of view, the system maintainer's view, or the user's view. None of these approaches will make the computer any smarter than any of the others, although in certain applications it may appear as though the computer is smarter than it appears in others, depending upon the approach utilized.

The critical decisions that must be made, then, are in many ways the typical questions that one asks when designing any system: what is its desired function? From the researcher's point of view, the function might be to act on data in new and different ways. For the average computer user, it might be to anticipate the user's requirements, to respond more quickly, or to respond in a language that is closer to a natural language. For the system maintainer, it might be to have a representation that is easiest for *them* to comprehend, so that changes in the future can be easily and accurately made.

SUMMARY

The task of designing a knowledge representation scheme for any system that hopes to make use of artificial intelligence is one that has a critical importance. Ultimately, the style, format, and assumptions inherent in any knowledge representation scheme will have a pervasive impact on what can and cannot be encoded, processed, and ultimately accomplished with the system. As will be demonstrated in later chapters, this task is at times so obvious that ignoring it is difficult, as with expert systems. It is an issue that suffuses all of the work being done in artificial intelligence and will in all likelihood have an impact on the field of computer science in general.

Graph Search

As we have seen, there is a great deal of interest in programs that use artificial intelligence; somehow they can appear magic, or threatening, or both. No one would think of calling a payroll program an AI application: AI brings to mind the leading edge of technology, "smart" computers, and the wave of the future; payroll programs instead conjure up images of punched cards, vacuum tubes, and paper tape.

Despite these differences, however, an AI program remains, at its heart, a computer program, essentially no different in content than the dullest payroll application. Both the expert system and the payroll program store data and programs in a series of bits; both interact with the world through an array of peripheral devices, using standard cables, and interfaces; both must store and retrieve information using a set of standard procedures (probably via the operating system). The contradiction, then, is that an AI program is "just" a program, yet it clearly makes use of ideas and strategies in such a way as to perform faster, more "humanly," and more flexibly, over a certain class of problems. To what can we attribute this difference?

As we have seen previously, the problem of knowledge representation is a crucial one, as it affects the speed, power, and even "flavor" of the AI application that is ultimately produced. This last factor is much more the case in AI applications than in traditional programs, primarily due to the fact that traditional applications need not be particularly worried about the nuances of how the data appears to people, whether at input or output. Yet this data is stored in a physical form that is not, in principle, any different than the form in which "knowledge" for AI programs is stored. Clearly, the difference is in the *organization* of knowledge. What are these methods of knowledge organization on a "lower" level? For an answer to this, we must explore the world of trees and graphs.

In mathematics, when one speaks of *trees* and *graphs*, these terms are used differently than in everyday English. Both trees and graphs refer to collections of objects, or data, that bear some relationship to each other. The graph is the more general case, and can be most easily thought of as a road map, as shown in Fig. 4-1.

Now each of the stars in the above graph is known as a *node*, and it is "at" these nodes that the object, or data item, resides. The lines connecting the nodes, or *arcs*, may also have data items associated with them. To use the map analogy, each of the nodes could be used to identify a city, and numeric values could be assigned to each of the arcs to indicate the distance between the cities.

It is not, however, necessary to have values assigned to the arcs; if we were not concerned with distances, but were simply interested in which cities were connected by interstate highways, then we would not label the arcs at all. It is all up to the person designing the knowledge base, in AI terms, to determine what the nodes and arcs represent, and which types of data they will "carry."

Note that in the above example nodes may have one or more arcs associated with them, and thus may be connected to one or more other nodes. There are no particular rules about which nodes may be connected to which

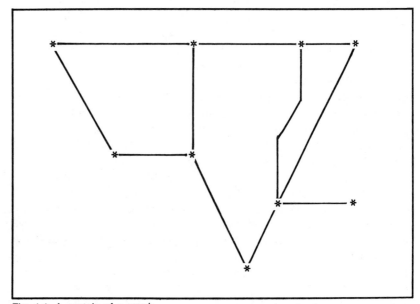

Fig. 4-1. A sample of a graph.

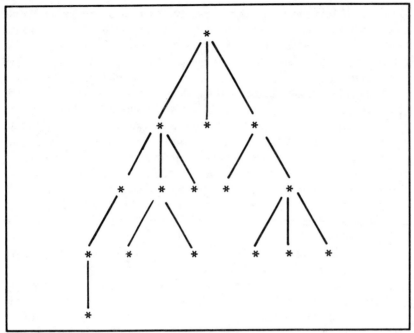

Fig. 4-2. A tree.

other nodes or how many nodes may be connected to a particular node. In trees, however, more rules apply.

In the example shown in Fig. 4-2, imagine that you have drawn a child's figure of a tree, and then turned it upside down. The point at the very top of the picture would be the root, and the leaves would be at the bottom. This is in fact the precise terminology that is used to describe the nodes of a tree, along with some geneological terms thrown in for good measure.

In a tree, the relative vertical position of each node is important, much in the same way that positions are important in family trees. A node that is connected by an arc to a lower node is called that lower node's *parent*; the lower node is the upper node's *child*. Children that are not themselves parents are known as *leaves*; the single parent that has no parents of its own (found at the top of the tree) is known as the *root*.

There are, therefore, more rules about trees than there are about graphs: a child can have only one parent, while a parent may have any number of children; there can only be one root to a tree, but there can be an indefinite number of children. This implies that children cannot be connected to each other, only to parents. Finally, there are special cases of trees that limit the number of children a parent can have; the most common is the *binary* tree, in which a parent may have only one or two children.

Before we discuss which situations are better suited to trees, graphs, or other strategies, let us examine how the information is retrieved from them, as this will have a direct bearing on the choice that we ultimately make. For clarity's sake, we will begin with the tree, as there is a direct relationship between the restrictiveness of a structure and the ease of retrieving information from it (as well as an inverse relationship between its restrictiveness and the richness of information that can be stored there).

Using the example of a binary tree as the most restrictive form of tree, we will attempt to "visit" each of the nodes of the tree in an orderly manner: that is, via a set of rules that a computer could follow.

A binary tree, you will recall, is one in which each parent can have only two or fewer children. There are several methods of traversing these trees; we will use what is known as *postfix*, as the tree has been drawn with this method in mind. An explanation of the term *postfix* and its relatives, *prefix* and *infix*, can be found at the end of this chapter for the curious.

The principles used in the postfix approach are that children are always visited before their parents, and that the left child is visited before the right. Thus, Tree 1 in Fig. 4-3 would be traversed in such a way as to yield the phrase "the blue sky."

In traversing this simple tree, we start at the root, *sky*, and visit its children, *the* and *blue*, before visiting it. Since the left child is always visited first, the resulting phrase is "the blue sky."

Now, expanding on the notion that children are to be visited before their parents, examine Tree 2 in Fig. 4-3.

If we start at the root, *pretty*, we try to visit its left child, *sky*. However,

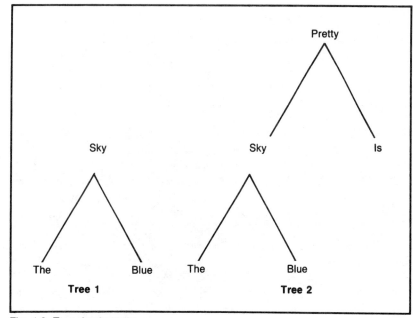

Fig. 4-3. Two simple trees.

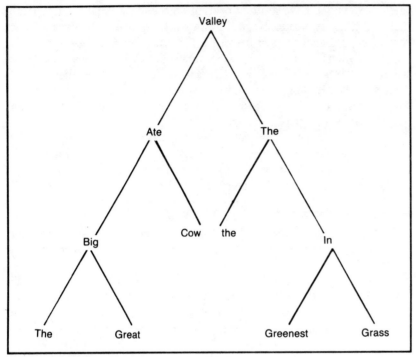

Fig. 4-4. Apply the rules of transversal to this tree.

sky has children: *the* and *blue*, so we must visit them before we visit *sky*, just as we did above. So we descend another *generation*, or *level*, down the tree, and visit *the*. Finding that it has no children, we then visit its sibling, *blue*, then finally the parent, *sky*. Next, we examine the sibling of *sky, is,* and find that it has no children, so we visit it. Finally, we visit the parent of *is, pretty*, which also happens to be the root, and so we stop. The phrase generated by the above tree therefore reads, "the blue sky is pretty."

If you will follow the above strategy, you should be able to successfully generate the correct phrase from the tree in Fig. 4-4.

The correct phrase here is "the great big cow ate the greenest grass in the valley." If you generated something else, go over the examples above until you can correctly come up with the phrase given, remembering that children are always visited before parents, first left then right, and if a child has children, then its children must be visited first.

In traditional programming, how would one represent the rules of this traversal? It turns out to be rather complex, if one uses a language that does not allow for *recursion*, such as BASIC, COBOL, or FORTRAN. Under such circumstances, the rules, or algorithm, of the search become quite convoluted. The reason for this is that the natural language algorithm reads like this:

ALGORITHM: "POSTFIX VISIT"

Examine a node:

> If it has a left child, apply the algorithm "POSTFIX VISIT" to that child.
>
> If it has a right child, apply the algorithm "POSTFIX VISIT" to that child.
>
> If it has no children, or all its children have been visited, then print its value.

Since we invoke the algorithm within the algorithm itself, this makes the definition of the algorithm *recursive*; it refers to itself. Languages such as C, Pascal, and the AI languages all make use of recursion, and so for a program to traverse a binary tree in these languages is straightforward. This is especially true in the AI languages, since the programmer does not have to worry much about the way in which the tree is represented inside the computer. In languages that do not support recursion, however, the effort required is of major proportions.

Let us now examine a richer tree structure and compare its appearance with that of the binary tree's. We will use the same sentence as before, but this time we will allow more than two offspring to belong to a given parent, as shown in Fig. 4-5.

It should be apparent that, with a little work, it would be possible to derive a structure that is similar, if not identical, to the sentence graphs

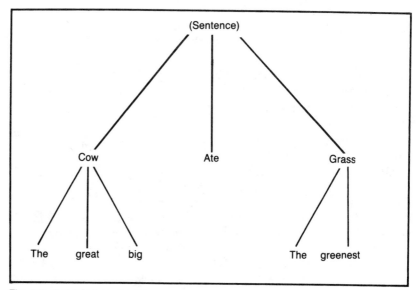

Fig. 4-5. A richer tree structure.

used by teachers a number of years ago. In fact, it is just this approach (in principle) that is used in trying to understand natural language: first the computer is given the task of figuring out the structure of the sentence, representing it as some form of a graph. Then the program can take the particular words stored at each node of the graph and try to generate some "understanding" from them.

There is another type of tree to be searched: the *game* tree. A game tree is structurally similar to any other mathematical tree, but there is one significant difference: instead of there being simply one person or one program attempting to search the tree, using one consistent algorithm (or set of algorithms), there are two (or more) parties involved in the search. And, as the notation of "game" implies, these parties are in competition with each other and may not even be using the same set of algorithms. We will briefly explore one of the classic types of game tree search and then move on to a programming exercise to allow for dynamic memory management: a much-needed facility when you are searching trees and graphs.

MINIMAX SEARCH

One of the techniques used for searching game trees is that of the *MiniMax* search. It attempts to reduce the amount of search time and storage space required by developing only a portion of the tree to be searched. Its ultimate aim is a pessimistic (or perhaps realistic) one: it finds the node that has the characteristic of being the one from which the least detrimental subtree can be developed.

MiniMax is based on the presumption that each player has equally effective methods of evaluating each move, although this is not a prerequisite for its use. It furthermore makes the common sense assumption that each player will make the best move available to them, in the sense that each would, given the choice, pick the move that scored the highest on its evaluation.

The term MiniMax is derived from the notion that each player will play defensively; that is, it will attempt to *mini*mize the opponent's *max*imum game. An example will serve to clarify this approach:

Let us presume that player one, Alpha, is a computer, playing a game against a human competitor, Beta. At each move, Alpha will evaluate the position of the checkers on the board by examining all the moves possible within a given limit; let us say for example, the next two moves ahead. Each possible move will be scored for its relative merit and will be rendered as nodes in a graph for ease of choice. Alpha's scoring function is such that it will find the highest score to be the best for it; conversly, the lowest score for a given position will be the best for Beta (the human competitor).

Let us imagine a game in which for any position, there are three moves possible, and Alpha will look two moves in advance; that is, it will examine its three available moves and the nine responses to them. Tree 1 in Fig.

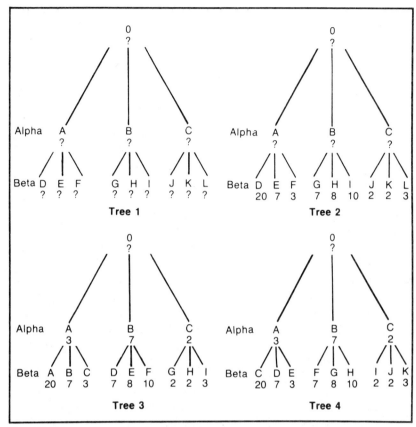

Fig. 4-6. Trees with assigned values.

4-6 is an unscored graph of this situation; letters represent the possible moves, and the question marks will be replaced with scores once the evaluation function has been performed on each node.

Thus, Alpha is going to make a move; it will examine each of its three moves—A, B, and C—in order to decide which move to make. In doing so, Alpha will examine each of Beta's possible responses to those moves: for A: D, E, and F; and so on. It will do so by, let us say, a depth-first search of the tree, accomplished by expanding first node A, then node B, and finally C. As it develops each of the children to A, B, and C, it will use its evaluation function to determine the relative merit of each position, and then place that value at the corresponding node of the tree. Let us presume that the nine leaves have been evaluated and entered into the tree as shown in Tree 2 in Fig. 4-6.

Recall that Alpha's best scores are the highest ones, and that Beta's scores are the lowest. This means that Beta, given the choice, will always choose the lowest score available to it. Since the nine leaves represent choices to Beta, let us assign the lowest-valued child's score to its parent, since Beta would certainly make the best move that it could. Such a "percolation" of scores would yield Tree 3 in Fig. 4-6.

Now Alpha wants to take the best move available to it, which is represented by the *largest* score. So, of the available choices—3, 7, and 2—it will choose the largest, 7, or move B. This would yield the final tree, Tree 4 in Fig. 4-6.

Translating this strategy into a more natural form, we can see that we have adopted a very conservative stance: Move A, evaluated finally as 3, had the greatest potential outcome, 20. However, the MiniMax function worked against it, preferring to take the absolutely safest route possible. This may in fact be the best overall strategy to pursue, as long as the hidden assumptions are recognized and accepted:

First, it is assumed that the evaluation function is a valid and effective one; perhaps a trivial-sounding assumption, but an important one nonetheless: the computer will only generate a result that is as good as the heuristic behind it.

Secondly, we are making the assumption that the other player, in this case Beta, will not make any mistakes; in particular, we are assuming that he will see all the moves that we see. Thus, we will abandon the more risky venture in the example above because, as part of our assumption, there can be no risk, either for us or against us: both players can see the same situation, and they see it equally well.

The only thing that prevents this model of a game from becoming completely predictable from the first move is that each player, presumably, can only look a finite number of moves ahead, and that number is less than the total number of moves in the game. Indeed, if it were possible to plot every alternative, then a strategy such as the MiniMax search would not be necessary.

ALPHA-BETA PRUNING

A further refinement to the MiniMax strategy is that of Alpha-Beta pruning. This is a procedure that was developed as a way of optimizing the MiniMax search, and it embodies what appears to be a good deal of common sense.

First developed in 1968 by Slagle and Dixon, the procedure gets its name from AI work that was being done by them in regards to game strategies. They had been using two programs, which they had code-named Alpha and Beta, and were using the MiniMax function described above to conduct the overall operation of the system.

The notion behind Alpha-Beta pruning is actually quite straightforward: one does not expand a node if it can be seen from early on that it will not be productive (from a MiniMax perspective), and in fact one stops expanding a node *as soon* as it becomes unpromising. For example, let us take

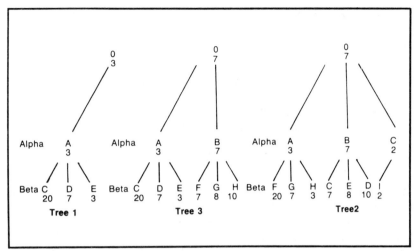

Fig. 4-7. Trees with assigned values.

the tree that we were developing above, and presume that it was developed in a right-to-left order. Recall the final tree in Fig. 4-6. Remember that the MiniMax approach is going to look for the largest number at the Alpha level for its move. Furthermore, the values at that level are the *smallest* values of the children for each node, or the values at the Beta level. Tree 1 in Fig. 4-7 shows what the tree would look like after the first node is expanded. Notice that we have *percolated*, or propagated, the smallest Beta value up to A: E's value of 3. Likewise, since there are no other children as yet, we have propagated the value 3 up to 0, as the best value so far.

Now refer to Tree 2 in Fig. 4-7 to see what expanding the B node does. Here, we have been able to send the value 7 up to 0, as it was the smallest of B's children, but larger than the value passed upwards by A (3). So far, the procedure has been identical to that of the example above, but study Tree 3 in Fig. 4-7 to see what happens as we begin to expand node C. We will take each of C's children in succession, for the clearest illustration.

First we evaluate node I, and determine that it has a value of 2. We can pass this up to C, and upon comparing it with 0's value of 7, find it to be smaller. This tells us that there is no point in expanding C any further, as the *largest* value that we could possibly generate would be a 2 (since Beta will always choose the lowest number available), and this value is less than our best choice so far, 7. Since we are always going to choose the largest number available to us, we can ignore the remainder of C, and either continue on to other nodes (if any) or terminate the algorithm.

Note that the order in which nodes are evaluated can have a critical impact on the effectiveness of Alpha-Beta pruning (although it will never make it *worse* than MiniMax): had B been evaluated first, and then the children of A evaluated in reverse order, only B would have been fully evaluated. Conversely, had B been evaluated last, and C first, then all the nodes would have had to have been evaluated in order to complete the search.

MEMORY MANAGEMENT AND GRAPH SEARCH

In order to be able to process the large volumes of information usually found in trees and graphs, it becomes critical to be able to create nodes to these graphs in a dynamic manner, adding and subtracting them from the tree whenever necessary. Furthermore, since many of the nodes may only be used on a temporary basis, it would be nice if it were not necessary to reserve enough room for all possible graphs at the beginning of the program, but instead to allocate memory for the program as the need arose, shifting more in when necessary, releasing other portions when they were no longer required.

This type of approach is easiest to accomplish in languages like LISP, Pop-11, and Prolog, since they manage memory dynamically and thus can conduct their processing in a more space-efficient manner. Since this amounts to maintaining a system that mimics the purposes of the operating system (resource management), it usually results in slower processing and, paradoxically, a potentially larger overhead.

Other languages give the user the opportunity to dynamically manage memory at a lower level through the use of *pointers*, or values that indicate the location in the computer's memory where the contents of variables are actually stored. Such programming languages (such as Pascal and 'C'), while they give the user the opportunity to manage these resources more precisely, also give rise to the opportunity for users to make mistakes and either damage the functioning of their program or perhaps even corrupt portions of memory that are not theirs to have access to.

It is for this reason that programs making use of these facilities are usually either reserved for advanced programmers or used as teaching aids in highly controlled environments. In the remainder of this chapter, we will examine a method by which memory can be managed on a pseudo-dynamic basis via the BASIC language, which is not particularly suited to this type of processing. Such an exercise, however, gives an appreciation for the issues involved in high-level programming and will also serve as a foundation for other programs in this text that require dynamic memory management but are written in BASIC so that they may be run on a home computer.

This section presents a scheme by which memory allocation can be made available in a BASIC environment and as such gives a glimpse into the internals of how AI programs can accomplish some of the feats that they do. It will not be necessary to complete this section in order to follow the other material in the book; however, the other BASIC programs provided will operate within an abbreviated version of the environment detailed here. The environment ultimately built will be neither elegant nor efficient; it will, however, be functional.

The first problem to be addressed is how to reserve and access memory from within a BASIC program. While BASIC provides the functions PEEK and POKE for the purpose of accessing memory, reserving it is another problem. Since the manner of accomplishing this is variant across different implementations of BASIC, we will utilize a method which operates by brute force. As a result, we will restrict ourselves to two data types: integers and characters, which are essentially the same thing. Strings of fixed length will be possible, and the clever user will be able to generate variable-length strings from this notion. Real numbers are indeed possible as well, but they are beyond the scope of this exercise and are left to the truly ambitious programmer.

The simplest manner of reserving memory in BASIC is to dimension an array of integers, as this yields both a fixed store of memory and an access into each element of it. Another advantage of using integers is that the ASCII values of characters can be stored there in a manner that is transparent to the user. Therefore, one of the first statements within our BASIC environment will be to establish a large array of integers of a size that can be varied to suit the specific resources of the computer. We will then divide this space into three sections: the first block, the middle block, and the last block. Memory that is required will always be obtained from the middle block and will be returned there by the user when it is no longer in use.

The reason for restricting the user's memory to the central block is that, by using some methods of "tricking" the algorithms that are used to obtain and return memory, we can easily avoid problems that may arise from looking for memory outside the bounds that we have established. We will examine these tricks in a bit; first, we must investigate the general approach that we will use for obtaining and returning memory.

Each block of usable memory (as well as the first and last blocks) will

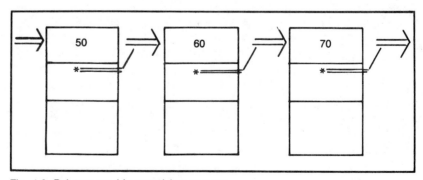

Fig. 4-8. Pointers used in organizing memory.

be organized according to the following system: the first integer in the block will the size of the block, and the second will be a pointer to the next free block (in actuality, the index number of the next free space in the array). Thus, if we had three free blocks with 50, 60, and 70 being "free" integers, respectively, we could graphically represent the storage as shown in Fig. 4-8.

The strategy that is used in this program is that whenever a certain amount of memory is requested by the user, the first available space that is greater than or equal to the amount requested is found by "walking" down the list of available space. If the amount matches exactly, then the entire chunk is returned to the user. If the block is larger, however, the amount required is "sliced" from the "bottom" of the block, primarily so that the chain of blocks can remain unbroken. All that will be required in this case is that the size parameter (found in the first element of the block) be adjusted downward to reflect the loss.

When memory is returned, it is "absorbed" back into the available free list as neatly as possible. Thus, if the "top" of the returned chunk is adjacent to the "bottom" of another chunk, the first chunk (the one already on the list) will simply have its size parameter adjusted upwards to reflect the recent acquisition. Likewise, if the bottom of the returned chunk is adjacent to the top of another chunk already on the list, then the block already present will be absorbed into the newly returned block.

There are a number of "tricks" that are played with this scheme, all of which help it to function more efficiently and with less involvement from the user. The first is that, in actuality, the user never "sees" the true pointer at the beginning of the block: the system returns the index of the *next* slot to the user as if it were the first. The reason for this is that this removes the responsibility of maintaining the index of the block (for its later return to the free list) from the user and allows the program to manage this book-keeping.

The other set of tricks revolves around the manner in which the first and last blocks are maintained. The problem that can often arise is that special tests need to be performed when managing a list that have to do with testing for the first and last elements of that list. For example, when trying to absorb a chunk back into the list, if that chunk happened to be the first, you would have to make certain that the program did not try and meld it with a previous block. Similarly, if the block was the last, the program would have to be secured against attempting to meld past the end of the list.

The general strategy, then, is to make certain that all blocks of memory are obtained from and returned to the middle of the list. We can ensure this by making the first and last blocks inaccessible, which is accomplished like this:

Both the first and last blocks are purposely set up with size parameters of zero; this way, they will never be large enough to be allocated to a user.

This takes care of half of the problems, in that these blocks will never leave the free list. The remaining problem is to make certain that other blocks are never melded with the first and last blocks.

This is accomplished by setting the pointers to the blocks after the first and as far as the one just before the last, such that an extra "space" is left between the first and middle, and the middle and last. Thus, by only wasting two slots, the first and last slots are guaranteed never to be next to a returned block, and hence will never be melded to it.

The program that follows is documented sufficiently that the methods used in accomplishing these goals should be clear. The program is designed to be placed before the beginning of a user program, which will always begin at line 3000.

The Dynamic Memory Allocation Program

```
1000 '
1001 '              Dynamic Memory Allocation Scheme
1002 '                 (c) James F. Brule' 1986
1003 '
1004 DEFINT A-Z:'      Force all data to be integers
1005 '
1006 '               By convention, all "system" variables will
1007 '                  start with the letter "Q"
1008 '
1009 QMAX=5000:'       Set size for memory to be allocated
1010 '
1011 DIM QRAM(QMAX):'  Actually allocate memory
1012 '
1013 '
1014 '               Memory mapping follows this system:
1015 '               The first integer in each block is the size
1016 '                  of the block;
1017 '               The second integer is a pointer to the start
1018 '             •    of the next block;
1019 '
1020 QNEXT=1:'         Provides automatic index to size parameter
1021 '
1022 '               The first block is QTOP; it has a declared size
1023 '                  of 0, and points to the first usable block,
1024 '                  leaving a gap of 1 integer to prevent
1025 '                  melding of it with usable blocks. Thus, the
1026 '                  first usable block begins at QRAM(3).
1027 QTOP=0
```

```
1028 QRAM(QTOP)=0:'            Its size
1029 QRAM(QTOP+QNEXT)=3:'   Pointer to next block
1030 '
1031 '                The last block is QBOT; it has a declared size
1032 '                    of 0, and has a null pointer (-1) to
1033 '                    identify it as the last block. It also has a
1034 '                    single element gap between the bottom of the
1035 '                    last usable block, to prevent its being
1036 '                    melded into the usable memory space.
1037 '
1038 QBOT=QMAX-1:'            Its location
1039 QRAM(QBOT)=0:'            Its size
1040 QRAM(QBOT+QNEXT)=-1:'   Its pointer to the next block
1041 '
1042 '                The first usable block is set up to occupy all
1043 '                    of available memory.
1044 '                First, we make sure QTOP points to it:
1045 QFIRST=QRAM(QTOP+QNEXT)
1046 '                Then, we set its size to equal the maximum
1047 '                    available (QMAX) less the amount required
1048 '                    for QTOP and its gap ( QRAM(QTOP+QNEXT) ) and
1049 '                    the amount for QBOT and its gap (3):
1050 QRAM(QFIRST)=QMAX-QRAM(QTOP+QNEXT)-3
1051 '                        Finally, we link its pointer to QBOT:
1052 QRAM(QFIRST+QNEXT)=QBOT
1053 '
1054 GOTO 1228:'      We skip over the following functions; the user
1055 '                    program will reside at line 1228 forward.
1056 '
1057 '                SUBROUTINE QGET( QREQ, QADDR )
1058 '                    This subroutine obtains memory from the free
1059 '                    and returns it to the program. Two parameters
1060 '                    are used:
1061 '                QREQ - the amount of memory required;
1062 '                QADDR - the beginning address of the memory
1063 '                    provided.
1064 '
1065 '                It is the responsibility of the user to
1066 '                    maintain both these parameters, as they will
1067 '                    be needed when the memory is returned to the
1068 '                    free list. Furthermore, in order for the
1069 '                    need to know its location. However, since
1070 '                    these are system variables, these values
1071 '                    should be stored in a user variable
```

```
1072 '                        immediately upon return from the subroutine.
1073 '
1074 QTEST = QTOP:'   Set a test pointer to the top of the free
1075 '                  list; recall that it will never be a big
1076 '                  enough block, as its size is 0.
1077 '
1078 '                  Begin a loop searching for the first block which
1079 '                  is large enough to fill the request; when the
1080 '                  search is successful, exit the loop:
1081 IF QRAM(QTEST) >= QREQ THEN 1111
1082 '                  Since the test was unsuccessful, we must look at
1083 '                  the next block in the list. In order to
1084 '                  maintain the list, though, we need to know
1085 '                  where we came from. So the first step is to
1086 '                  establish a pointer to our original position:
1087 QORG = QTEST
1088 '                  Next, we move our test pointer one more block
1089 '                  down the list:
1090 QTEST = QRAM(QTEST+QNEXT)
1091 '                  If by some misfortune we are looking for a chunk
1092 '                  of memory that is simply too large given our
1093 '                  current resources, we will reach the end of
1094 '                  the free list. In this case, we have to fail
1095 '                  gracefully. So, first we test to see if we've
1096 '                  reached the end of the list:
1097 IF QTEST > 0 THEN 1081
1098 '                  If we have reached the end, we set a system
1099 '                  parameter,
1100 QERROR = 1
1101 '                  then return. It is therefore the user's
1102 '                  responsibility to check for this error every
1103 '                  time they request memory resources.
1104 RETURN
1105 '
1106 '                  We have found a block that is large enough to
1107 '                  meet the request. First, we test to see if
1108 '                  it is exactly the right size, as this will
1109 '                  have a bearing on how we maintain the free
1110 '                  list:
1111 IF QRAM(QTEST) > QREQ THEN 1128
1112 '                  It matches exactly! This means that we can just
1113 '                  point the block before the one we are going
1114 '                  to use to the one after it:
1115 QRAM(QORG+QNEXT) = QRAM(QTEST+QNEXT)
```

```
1116 '                    Next, we store the "address" of the block in
1117 '                        QADDR, for the user program to have:
1118 QADDR = QTEST
1119 '                    And then return.
1120 RETURN
1121 '
1122 '                    Since the block was too big, we only want to use
1123 '                        part of it. We will essentially chop off the
1124 '                        bottom of the block, so that the only change
1125 '                        we have to make in the free list is to update
1126 '                        size of the block we have used. The first
1127 '                        step is to alter that size paramter:
1128 QRAM(QTEST) = QRAM(QTEST)-QREQ
1129 '                    Then we calculate the beginning of the chunk
1130 '                        that we will return, by adding the size of
1131 '                        the block to the address of its top:
1132 QADDR = QTEST+QRAM(QTEST)
1133 '                    And finally return, having stored the address in
1134 '                        QADDR.
1135 RETURN
1136 '
1137 '
1138 '                    SUBROUTINE QPUT ( QREQ, QADDR )
1139 '
1140 '                    This subroutine returns memory to the free list,
1141 '                        doing some maintenance of the free list along
1142 '                        the way. It requires the same two parameters
1143 '                        as before, so that it knows how to maintain
1144 '                        the free list.
1145 '
1146 '
1147 '                    The first step is to find the block before and
1148 '                        after the block being returned. In order to
1149 '                        do this, we will have to follow the list
1150 '                        until we find a block that is further down
1151 '                        than QADDR, all the time maintaining a
1152 '                        pointer to the block we were just at (QLOW),
1153 '                        so that we can remember the block before the
1154 '                        one we are returning.
1155 '
1156 '                    The first step is to begin at the top of the
1157 '                        free list with QLOW:
1158 QLOW = QTOP
1159 '                    Next, we set the test pointer (QHI) to the first
```

```
1160 '              usable block:
1161 QHI = QRAM(QTOP+QNEXT)
1162 '
1163 '              Now we enter the loop to search for the right
1164 '              block:
1165 IF QHI > QADDR THEN 1175
1166 '              Since the above test failed, we must look
1167 '              further down the list. We start by moving the
1168 '              low pointer up to the high one:
1169 QLOW = QHI
1170 '              Then, we move the high pointer to the beginning
1171 '              of the next block:
1172 QHI = QRAM(QHI+QNEXT)
1173 '              And then loop:
1174 GOTO 1165
1175 '
1176 '              Now, QLOW points to the block before the one we
1177 '              are returning, and QHI to the block after.
1178 '              Our first task is to insert the block we are
1179 '              returning into the free list. We do this by
1180 '              setting the size parameter to the size of the
1181 '              block we are returning:
1182 QRAM(QADDR) = QREQ
1183 '              Next, we let the returned block point to the
1184 '              next block in the free list:
1185 QRAM(QADDR+QNEXT) = QHI
1186 '              And, likewise, let the block before the one we
1187 '              are returning point to the returned block:
1188 QRAM(QLOW+QNEXT) = QADDR
1189 '
1190 '              The next important task is to maintain the free
1191 '              free list. We will do this in two stages:
1192 '              first, check to see if the bottom of the
1193 '              returned block is adjacent to the top of the
1194 '              next block; if so, we will "meld" them into
1195 '              one block.
1196 '
1197 '              We test for this condition by comparing the
1198 '              address of the first entry after the returned
1199 '              block to that of the first entry of the next
1200 '              block:
1201 IF QADDR+QRAM(QADDR) < QHI THEN 1215
1202 '              Our test indicates that we should meld the
1203 '              blocks. To do this, we first add their two
```

57

```
1204 '                      sizes, and store the result in the returned
1205 '                      block:
1206 QRAM(QADDR) = QRAM(QADDR) + QRAM(QHI)
1207 '              Then we let the returned block point to the
1208 '              block that the higher block had been pointing
1209 '              to:
1210 QRAM(QADDR+QNEXT) = QRAM(QHI+QNEXT)
1211 '
1212 '              Now we perform the same test, this time
1213 '              comparing the bottom of the lower block with
1214 '              with the top of the returned block:
1215 IF QLOW+QRAM(QLOW) < QADDR THEN RETURN
1216 '              Again, we need to meld, so first we adjust the
1217 '              pointer of the lower block to point to the
1218 '              block that the returned block had been
1219 '              pointing to:
1220 QRAM(QLOW+QNEXT) = QRAM(QADDR+QNEXT)
1221 '              Finally, we adjust the size parameter of the
1222 '              lower block to account for the new space:
1223 QRAM(QLOW) = QRAM(QLOW) + QRAM(QADDR)
1224 '              The job complete, we now return to the user
1225 '              program:
1226 RETURN
1227 '
1228 ' User program begins with this line...
```

Programming
Languages for Artificial Intelligence

The field of artificial intelligence has generated a number of languages, all designed to facilitate the process of developing programs that make use of or test artificial intelligence in a more efficient manner. We will examine three of the most common languages used in AI today: LISP, Prolog, and Pop-11.

If you are writing artificial intelligence programs in the United States today, chances are you are writing in one of the many dialects of LISP. If, however, you are writing in Europe or Japan, the chances are that you are programming in Prolog. And if you are writing these programs in Great Britain or in a growing number of sites in Europe and the US you might be programming in Pop-11 or one of its precursors.

Of the three languages, two bear a functional resemblance to each other: LISP and Pop-11. These are known as list processing languages because they operate on lists of objects, rather than perform the traditional function of processing data. (LISP gets its name from this fact: LISt Processing; Pop-11 is named after one of its originators, Popplestone.)

Prolog is a very different language, in that its function is to support logic programming (and hence its name). Like LISP and Pop-11, Prolog operates on objects, but instead focuses on their logical relatedness, as opposed to their properties as members of lists. As a result, it has an entirely different flavor and set of applications than do list-processing languages.

Before we explore the attributes of each of these languages, it is useful to note the reason for having languages specifically devoted to artificial intelligence. After all, since all computer programs can ultimately be reduced to a series of ones and zeroes, what difference does the language make? Why should someone take the time to learn yet another language—especially one that appears as cryptic to the novice as LISP does—when other languages are available and known so well by so many? And, to take the point even further, languages for artificial intelligence are usually notorious for their lack of speed when it comes to numeric processing: could there be any reason to give up this facility, when much of artificial intelligence appears to be wrapped up in mathematical computations?

The answer, obviously, is that these languages *do* serve a set of purposes that are useful, and some even manage to get around the problems of numeric processing speed through special hardware or through carefully tailored programming environments. But what are the advantages to using these languages and how are they suited to artificial intelligence?

One of the styles of programming that has evolved out of the world of artificial intelligence is the notion of *prototyping*: the building of smaller, similarly functioning models of the ultimate end product. These models can be tested for logical fitness, functionality, and so on without having to build a major system. While this notion is known to many engineering disciplines, the notion of prototyping in software engineering has reached its pinnacle in artificial intelligence. And this is one of the greatest advantages that an AI language can give to its users.

As mentioned earlier, the AI languages operate on something called *objects,* rather than on *data*, the better-known entity. Philosophically, objects and data are the same entities, but functionally they are quite different. For example, in LISP the unit of processing is called an *atom*, and it may either be a number or more likely a word or list of words, in the everyday sense of the term. Thus, the LISP function:

```
(SETQ A '(THE QUICK BROWN FOX))
```

assigns the list, "THE QUICK BROWN FOX," to the atom A, by way of the function SETQ (set equal). Each of the items in this list can be addressed independently, through a variety of functions. If you wanted the first element of the list A, you would use the function:

```
(CAR A)
```

which would return:

```
THE
```

Or, if you wanted all but the first element, you would invoke the CDR function:

```
(CDR A)
```

```
(QUICK BROWN FOX)
```

The specific meanings of the terms and a more detailed look at the functions will be explored later in this chapter. For now, it is important to note the lack of effort required to retrieve these various elements. In other languages, the code for managing such operations would be substantial: one would have to set up a linked list of records, each one containing one of the words of the list, and manage the connections between them. Furthermore, there would have to be some sort of a *parser*, or translating function, to determine where one word ended and the next began.

But simply the ability to create prototype programs, while a major advantage, is not reason enough to pursue a new language; a *shell* of routines could be written to handle these functions, and standard calls could be developed to operate quickly and efficiently, probably without the loss of numeric processing capabilities. In fact, the simple memory management program for BASIC programs presented in Chapter 4 is the beginning of such a shell.

The critical difference between list processing languages and other, traditional programming languages is something that moves directly to the heart of the stereotype of the purpose of artificial intelligence as the development of thinking machines: programs written in these languages can write their own programs. Unlike other languages, LISP and Pop-11 do not draw firm lines between *program* and *data*. The lists of words and numbers generated by programs in these languages can therefore be programs in and of themselves, and these programs can generate further programs, and so on.

There is an analog in Prolog in that Prolog can also process lists, although it is not its primary function. Prolog's particular strength is being able to build and modify its own knowledge base (often called by the more traditional name, *database*, in Prolog) and influence its own logic through its own operation.

The AI languages also offer a variety of functions that serve to enhance the process of developing AI programs: for example, all of them possess the capability of *recursive* function calls: the ability of a function to call itself from within the program. Using Pop-11 as an example, let us see how such an ability might be useful:

There is a mathematical function known as *factorial*, written:

```
n!
```

where n is a number, and ! is the factorial function. Its primary use is in calculations involving probability theory and scheduling problems. It is calculated as follows: take every number, starting at 1, and multiply it by the next largest number, continuing upward until (and including) the number in question. Thus, 4! is equal to:

$$1 \times 2 \times 3 \times 4$$

or 24. 5! = $1 \times 2 \times 3 \times 4 \times 5$, or 120, and so on. Finally, for mathematical consistency, 0! is defined as being equal to 1.

Now, let us consider a more formal definition of the factorial function, and how this might be expressed in a language with recursive abilities: Upon closer examination, we could say that n! is the same thing as $(n-1)! \times n$; just as 5! was $4! \times 5$.

In Pop-11, the routine to calculate factorial would look something like this:

```
define factorial(n) -> result;
    if    n <= 0
    then  1 -> result
    else  n * factorial(n-1) -> result
    endif
enddefine;
```

And, for contrast, the LISP version (to be discussed later):

```
(DEFUN FACTORIAL (N)
       (COND (((<= N 0) 1)
             (T (* N (FACTORIAL (- N 1))))))))
```

The first line defines **factorial** as the name of the function, determines that the function will operate on the number supplied via **n**, and indicates that the answer will be placed in a variable called **result**. The next section says, in English: If n is less than or equal to zero, then the result is 1. If n is not less than or equal to zero, then the result is n × (n − 1)!. Finally, by way of the terms endif and enddefine, Pop-11 closes up shop.

The catch here is that there is a lot of housekeeping that goes on behind the scenes to make this happen. If we were to ask for the value of 3!, we would type:

```
factorial(3) =>
```

and get 6 as the result. Here is what would happen:

Pop-11 would check the value of the variable **n** and find that this was not less than or equal to zero (the "if" statement). It would therefore try and multiply 3 by factorial(2), only to discover that it now has to call **factorial** again to figure out what the value of 2! is. It would then put aside the calculation of 3! for a moment and start *another* execution of factorial, this time with **n** being equal to 2. Again, it would find 2 not less than or equal to zero, and so try and multiply 2 by factorial(1)—but now *another* execution is required! So this execution would also be set aside, and another run of factorial begun, this time with n equal to 1. As before, it would start up another run of factorial so that it could fulfill the requirement of multiplying 1 by factorial(0). This time, it would find a simple value for result, since the program tells us that factorial(0) = 1. So now the language passes the calculated value back up the chain of "sleeping" copies of factorial, in this manner:

Call	Action	Result
`factorial(0):`	`1 -> result`	`(1)`
`factorial(1):`	`1 x result -> result`	`(1)`
`factorial(2):`	`2 x result -> result`	`(2)`
`factorial(3):`	`3 x result -> result`	`(6)`

And 6 would be the final value stored in **result**, which would be printed out (or otherwise made available to the user).

One of the results of providing this type of *background housekeeping*—storing the copies of factorial as it recurses on itself and discarding them when they are through and so on—is that more is required of the language itself. Whereas most languages are either using a part of memory for the life of the program or not using it at all, recursive languages in general and AI languages in particular are constantly using portions of memory, discarding them later, and generally making a nuisance of themselves to the computer. So it becomes necessary for these languages to take matters of memory management into their own hands, as it were, and make certain that memory resources are returned to the system as soon as, but not until, they are no longer required. This process is called, colorfully, *garbage collection*, and all AI languages manage this process to one degree or another.

A final quality that has begun to emerge as a standard in AI languages is something called *incremental compiling*. Traditionally there have been two methods of translating a higher level language into the *machine code* (ones and zeros) that a computer operates on. Either the language was *interpreted*, meaning that each line of high level code was received by the *interpreter*, translated, and then executed one at a time; or it was *compiled*, meaning that the unit of translation was the entire program. The benefit of interpreted languages like BASIC was that you could stop a program while it was running, examine what the values of the variables were, make some changes, and resume execution, all without having to take the time to restructure the code or the system. This was ideal for prototyping, and in the beginning, all AI languages were interpreted for just these reasons. There are, however, prices you pay when you use an interpreted language: first of all, the program must be translated every time it is used, not just during development. This translating process slows down the execution speed significantly. Also, while using an interpreted language gives you a certain amount of flexibility, you lose the power of the computer to help you check for errors that are a result of either poor typing or poor logic, which is provided during the compiling process.

Incremental compiling is an attempt, largely successful, to combine these two approaches and receive the best of both worlds. It breaks down the final code into chunks, or *increments*, that are linked together (in a process that is invisible to the user) into a final piece of machine code. Because these increments are so small, it is possible to stop the execution of a program, as in an interpreted language, make changes, and recompile only those portions of the program that were actually changed. At present, there are versions of each of these languages that are incrementally compiled, although they tend to be those versions that run on computers larger than microcomputers.

Let us now take a look at each of the languages in some detail. We will begin with Pop-11, as it bears the strongest resemblance to traditional programming languages, then proceed to LISP, its cousin, and finally go on to Prolog.

POP-11

Pop-11 has its roots in a language called Pop, first written by Robin Popplestone and his colleagues for the Elliot 4130, and later enhanced and given the name Pop-2. (This language is described in a paper by Burstall, et al (1971) published by Edinburgh University.) After several metamorphoses, the language migrated to the University of Sussex, where it became known as Pop-11. There is speculation that the jump from version 2 to version 11 was simply a misinterpretation of the Roman numeral II as the Arabic numeral 11.

Pop-11 is a list-processing language, as mentioned before, with some rather useful features added on. It provides built-in pattern matching operators, vector and matrix operations, and the capability for writing concurrent programs—that is for writing things like operating systems or programs that must perform several tasks in a manner that appears to be simultaneously.

Pop-11 has a syntax that resembles the block-structured feel of languages like Pascal and PL/I. Perhaps its most obvious difference is that it makes assignments from the left to the right, unlike most programming languages. Thus, while in BASIC you would store the value 3 into variable N like this:

```
N = 3
```

in Pop-11, the statement looks like the following:

```
3 -> n;
```

Being a list processing language, Pop-11 has powerful functions for addressing the various elements of a list. For example, let us say that we have the following list:

```
[the quick brown fox] -> list1;
```

We could address the various items in the list as follows (the double asterisk indicates Pop-11's response):

```
list1(1) =>
** the

list1(2) =>
** quick

hd(list1) =>
** quick

tl(list1) =>
** [quick brown fox]
```

Notice that the first three lines yield an element of list1 as single elements, whereas the final line displays the "tail" (as opposed to the "head" in line three) of list1 as a list itself. Thus, if we did the following:

```
tl(list1) -> list2;
list2(2) =>
```

we would receive as a result:

```
** brown
```

Lists may be composed not only of simple elements, but also of other lists, as in:

```
[[the quick [brown fox]] jumped over [the lazy [red hen]]] -> sentence;
```

If we wanted the first element of the list, we could ask for the "head" of the list, which would result in:

```
hd(sentence) =>
** [the quick [brown fox]]

hd(hd(sentence)) =>
** the
```

We could also index into the list, as seen below. Both methods are essentially equivalent.

```
sentence(1) =>
** [the quick [brown fox]]

sentence(1)(1) =>
** the
```

Other operations that can be performed on lists include deleting an element from a list:

```
delete("seven", [one three five seven nine]) =>
** [one three five nine]
```

or selecting an item at random from a list:

```
oneof([how now brown cow]) =>
** brown
```

or reversing its order:

```
rev([this sentence is backwards]) =>
** [backwards is sentence this]
```

Lists can be added to, either by keeping the new elements as separate sublists:

```
[a e i o u] -> vowels;
[1 2 3 4 5] -> numerals;
[^vowels ^numerals] =>
** [[a e i o u] [1 2 3 4 5]]
```

or joining them into a single list:

```
[^^vowels ^^numerals] =>
** [a e i o u 1 2 3 4 5]
```

Furthermore, tests can be made about the nature of lists. For example, you can see if an element is contained in a list:

```
member("a", vowels) =>
** <true>
```

or see if a certain pattern of elements is in a list. If you wanted to test to see if the sequence "2 3 4" was in **numerals**, for example, the command would be:

```
numerals matches [== 2 3 4 ==] =>
** <true>
```

The symbol = = indicates any set of list elements, including no elements. Thus, we could query about the sequence "1 2 3" as follows:

```
numerals matches [== 1 2 3 ==] =>
** <true>
```

since the first = = would match to no elements, or the empty list.

These functions are all present, in one form or another, in LISP. One of the more striking differences between Pop-11 and LISP, from an appearance point of view, is the way that procedures are defined. In Pop-11, procedures resemble functions and procedures in more traditional languages, whereas in LISP they are (at first glance) much more cryptic. A Pop-11 procedure to print out each element of a list could be written as follows:

```
define printeach(list);
   vars list;
   until list = []
   do spr(hd(list));
      tl(list) -> list;
   enduntil;
enddefine;
```

The first line of the function, called **printeach**, indicates that it takes as input a list, called **list**. The second line declares the variable for use inside the program. Next follows the beginning of a loop that will continue to execute until the list is empty ([ ]). The end of this loop is at the line enduntil. The actions taken inside the loop are to print (spr) the head of the list, then assign the tail of the list to be the next list to operate on. In other words, the loop prints the first element, strips it off, then continues printing and stripping until there is nothing left.

There are many other features of Pop-11 that make it a useful language, but the above imparts a flavor of the types of operations you can perform in it, along with the way that such operations are likely to appear.

LISP

LISP, the major list processing language in the United States, was developed by John McCarthy in 1958, shortly after the appearance of FOR-TRAN. It remained the province of back-room programmers and did not start to gain any sort of widespread acceptance until recently. At present, there are many dialects of LISP available, the most noteworthy being Common LISP, which represents an attempt to develop a standard LISP throughout the US.

Functionally, LISP is quite similar to Pop-11, although it is more difficult to learn how to read and use. In fact, it is often referred to as standing for "Lots of Irritating Single Parentheses," the reason for which should become apparent.

Every statement in LISP is itself a list and is delimited by parentheses. As in Pop-11, a list may consist of single elements, a group of lists, or any combination of these. Thus, a program can be seen as a list of lists, each of which will be comprised of other lists and elements, and so on.

One of the quirks about LISP syntax is that it is written in what is known as *prefix* notation, as opposed to the more common *infix* notation. In order to write the operation 2 + 3, for example, in LISP you would write:

```
(+ 2 3)
== 5
```

The plus sign is the operation, and it comes before (*pre*) the operands, 2 and 3. All operations follow this format, which does has its advantages once you become accustomed to it. In order to add a list of numbers, since the same operation is to be performed on a continuing basis, it will be sufficient to mention the operation once:

```
(+ 2 3 4 5 6 1 9)
== 30
```

To perform the complicated calculation $(3 + 2) * (4 + 3) - 2$, the LISP syntax would be:

```
(- (* (+ 3 2) (+ 4 3)) 2)
== 33
```

The same list operations mentioned for Pop-11 are present in LISP. The *head* of a list is called the CAR, and the *tail* is called the CDR (having to do with the names of hardware registers originally used by McCarthy). The operations that correspond to the Pop-11 operations mentioned earlier are:

```
(SETQ LIST1 '(THE QUICK BROWN FOX))
== (THE QUICK BROWN FOX)

(CAR LIST1)
== QUICK

(CDR LIST1)
== (QUICK BROWN FOX)

(SETQ LIST2 (CDR LIST1))
== (QUICK BROWN FOX)

(SETQ SENTENCE JUMPED(RED '((THE QUICK(BROWN FOX))OVER(THELAZYHEN))))
== ((THE QUICK (BROWN FOX)) JUMPED OVER (THE LAZY (RED HEN)))

(CAR SENTENCE)
== (THE QUICK (BROWN FOX))

(CAR (CAR SENTENCE))
== THE

(CAAR SENTENCE)
= THE

(DELETE 'SEVEN '(ONE THREE FIVE SEVEN NINE))
== (ONE THREE FIVE NINE)

(REVERSE '(THIS SENTENCE IS BACKWARDS))
== (BACKWARDS IS SENTENCE THIS)

(SETQ VOWELS '(A E I O U))
== (A E I O U)
(SETQ NUMERALS '(1 2 3 4 5))
```

```
==  (1  2  3  4  5)

(LIST VOWELS NUMERALS)
==  ((A E I O U) (1 2 3 4 5))

(APPEND VOWELS NUMERALS)
==  (A E I O U 1 2 3 4 5)

(MEMBER 'A VOWELS)
==  T
```

Two other functions mentioned in the Pop-11 section, that of being able to match lists using *wildcards* (the = = sign, amongst others) and of being able to retrieve a random element from a list, are not supported directly, but procedures may be written to accommodate these needs.

Examining for a moment the manner in which functions are defined in LISP, let us compare the programs for factorial that were presented earlier:

Pop-11:

```
define factorial(n) -> result;
    if      n <= 0
    then  1 -> result
    else  n * factorial(n-1) -> result
    endif
enddefine;
```

Lisp:

```
(DEFUN FACTORIAL (N)
      (COND (((<= N 0) 1)
            (T (* N (FACTORIAL (- N 1))))))
```

The first line of the LISP program indicates that we are defining a function **factorial**, with the input value to be stored in **n**. The second line begins a *conditional* statement. A conditional has the following structure: following the keyword **COND** is a list of lists. The CAR of each list is an element (either an atom or a list) that will be assessed as to whether it is true (T) or not. If it is true, then the remainder of that list is executed, after which LISP moves to the next list *beyond* the COND list.

The first list following COND, then, is:

```
(((<= N 0) 1)
```

for which the CAR is (< = N 0), or the test, " is N less than or equal to 0?" If this is true, then 1 will be the result of this call to FACTORIAL.

The second (and final) list following COND is:

```
(T (* N (FACTORIAL (- N 1))))
```

The CAR of this list is T: in other words, it guarantees that if LISP gets this far, it will execute the remainder of this list.

The CDR of this list is a statement that multiplies N by the factorial of N-1—requiring a recursive call to factorial.

Notice the six parentheses at the end of the full function above. These are required because all the parentheses must be balanced in order for LISP to know that the function is complete. (Pop-11 knows this via the statement "enddefine.") Most versions of LISP allow a shortcut under these circumstances—the replacement of the final series of closing parentheses with a square bracket. Thus, the LISP function that made use of this facility would look like:

```
(DEFUN FACTORIAL (N)
    (COND (((<= N 0) 1)
        (T (* N (FACTORIAL (- N 1]
```

a much more readable line of code. Much of the time the programmer, however, will be looking for parentheses to keep balanced, which is why many of the LISP development environments provide automated tools to alert the programmer as to all unbalanced parentheses.

As a final note, two companies have developed machines that are dedicated to programming in LISP: Symbolics and LISP Machines Inc. (LMI). Each of these machines has an architecture that is dedicated to artificial intelligence in general and LISP in particular. By customizing their central processors to recognize LISP and providing large amounts of main and secondary memories, these companies have made it possible to develop LISP programs that are capable of performing even highly complex mathematical calculations rapidly. The drawback is that these machines are very expensive, and by and large are devoted to single users. Their primary purpose at this time is to support the highly advanced artificial intelligence research and development that takes place in the labs of the largest companies and government contractors.

PROLOG

Prolog, which derives its name from the term *logic programming*, was initially developed around 1970 and has engendered a number of variations in the intervening years. The most common implementation of Prolog is

Artificial Intelligence: Theory, Logic and Application

known as *Edinburgh Syntax* or *DEC-10* Prolog, after the work of Clocksin and Mellish at Edinburgh University. Whereas Pop-11 and LISP have their best applications in situations that require the processing of lists, Prolog is best suited for solving problems in which the nature of the problem can be described in terms of relationships between objects. Simple programs can be written quickly, establishing the facts, the relationships between the facts, and the operations upon those facts that are of interest to the user. Manipulating those facts in an attempt to discover the desired answers about their relationships is known as *instantiation*, a logical term meaning to find an instance or example of a fact to support a theory.

Let us imagine that we are trying to sort out some soap-opera-like gossip on a set of acquaintances that we have. We would first establish who likes whom, perhaps with the following:

```
likes(alan,betty).
likes(cindy,david).
likes(david,cindy).
likes(ellen,frank).
```

and so on. The *clauses* above indicate who likes whom, in the sense that the first clause says "alan likes betty." Note that these are one-directional relationships: alan likes betty, but betty may or may not like alan.

Next, we could establish dislikes:

```
hates(betty,cindy).
hates(alan,frank).
```

which are read as above: "betty hates cindy," and "alan hates frank." Then we need some rules about how these qualities interact:

```
hates(X,Y) :-   likes(X,Z),
                hates(Z,Y).
```

This clause says that X hates Y if X likes Z and Z hates Y. In other words, if you are my friend's enemy, then you are my enemy as well.

One question we might want to ask, having established all this, is who alan hates. We would phrase this as follows:

```
hates(alan,X).
   X=frank ;
   X=cindy ;
   no
```

This rather cryptic response is read as follows: first the user types in the first line, asking for an instance of the "hates" relationship in which alan is the first term. Prolog searches the collection of facts and relationships, known as the *database*, and discovers that if X = frank, the goal is met. So it prints out **X = frank** and waits for the user to respond. If the user responds with a semicolon, as above, then Prolog goes off and tries to meet the goal a second time. This time it returns **X = cindy**, and again the user prompts Prolog for another try. This time, there is no other relationship that meets the goal, and Prolog responds with **no**.

We also could have asked about who hates alan as follows:

```
hates(X,alan).
   no
```

We get the **no** response immediately, since there is no instance of anyone hating alan. If we had asked about frank, though, we would have seen:

```
hates(X,frank).
   X=alan ;
   no
```

Understanding the way that Prolog goes about arriving at these instantiations is central to developing an understanding of what Prolog is well-suited for. What happens is that Prolog accepts the goal from the user (which may either be interactive or part of a program) and then tries to find an instance of that goal being true. It does this by trying to "plug in" each item in the database into each variable in the goal, trying every combination until it either finds a solution or runs out of items. If it needs to expand a relationship, such as was done above, it will do so, exhaustively searching every possibility. If it cannot come up with a single instantiation, then it returns a **no** to the user. Otherwise, it returns the first instantiation it could find, in a sense marking that success so that, should the user require another attempt, it will not return the same instantiation twice.

The basic method used for searching the database is backward chaining. There is a degree of control that the programmer can exert over this process, but it is not as easily accomplished as it might be in other languages. The reason for this is that Prolog offers an invisible control strategy that provides the benefit of ease in programming; with that ease, however, comes the inevitable restriction in the degree of control that one can exert over the program in a simple manner.

The syntax of Prolog is somewhat straightforward to read, although it can be more difficult to write. A relationship is preceded by a term that serves as its label and followed by its operands, which are enclosed in parentheses. Terms that begin with a lower case letter are atoms, and those that begin with upper case letters are variables.

Artificial Intelligence: Theory, Logic and Application

The :- symbol stands for the if relationship, in the sense that the term to the left of the :- will be established in the database if what follows to the right is instantiated. Terms on the right hand side may be joined either by an AND function (the comma) or the OR function (the semicolon). For example, if I wanted to establish that anyone who was either my friend's friend or my enemy's enemy was my friend, I would say:

```
likes(X,Y) :- (likes(X,F),
               likes(F,Y)) ;
              (enemy(X,E),
               enemy(E,Y)).
```

You will notice that the ordering of functions and elements is much like the prefix notation of LISP: the operator comes first, and then the operands follow. In Prolog, you have the option of working in infix notation if you wish, by declaring an operator to be so.

If we examine in brief detail the program to ask questions about a family tree—a classic in the realm of demonstrating Prolog—we can see how some of these functions operate.

First we declare a set of operators, indicating that they will all be infix. In this set of commands, we indicate that the operator will fall between two operands by the portion xfx, where the f stands for the operator, and the xs stand for variables. Each operator is given a name, which will be used throughout the program. Notice, however, that the operators is__female and is__male are operators with a single operand.

Some of the operators will be:

```
:- op(200, yf,  is_male).
:- op(200, yf,  is_female).
:- op(200, xfx, is_a_parent_of).
:- op(200, xfx, is_a_child_of).
:- op(200, xfx, is_the_mother_of).
:- op(200, xfx, is_the_father_of).
:- op(200, xfx, is_a_son_of).
:- op(200, xfx, is_a_daughter_of).
:- op(200, xfx, is_married_to).
:- op(200, xfx, married).
:- op(200, xfx, is_a_grandparent_of).
:- op(200, xfx, is_a_sibling_of).
:- op(200, xfx, is_a_brother_of).
:- op(200, xfx, is_a_sister_of).
:- op(200, xfx, is_an_uncle_of).
```

Next, we will store the data we require into the database. You can re-

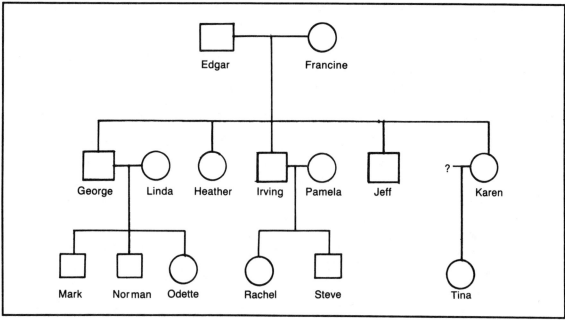

Fig. 5-1. A typical family tree.

fer to the family tree in Fig. 5-1 to decipher the database.

Here is the code for the data to be inserted into the database:

```
edgar is_male.
francine is_female.
francine married edgar.

george is_a_child_of edgar.
heather is_a_child_of edgar.
irving is_a_child_of edgar.
jeff is_a_child_of edgar.
karen is_a_child_of edgar.
X is_a_child_of francine :- X is_a_child_of edgar.
```

The above line is an effort-saving device: it simply assigns each child of edgar's to be a child of francince's. No second marriages here!

```
george is_male.
heather is_female.
irving is_male.
jeff is_male.
karen is_female.
```

```
linda is_female.
george married linda.
mark is_a_child_of linda.
norman is_a_child_of linda.
odette is_a_child_of linda.
X is_a_child_of george :- X is_a_child_of linda.

mark is_male.
norman is_male.
odette is_female.

pamela is_female.
irving married pamela.
rachel is_a_child_of irving.
steve is_a_child_of irving.
X is_a_child_of pamela :- X is_a_child_of irving.

rachel is_female.
steve is_male.

tina is_a_child_of karen.
tina is_female.
```

Finally, while this will not generate sufficient code to run the system, let us examine how the rules will be written to manage this database and then make a few inquiries into the system.

The first rule will define marriage as being a two-way street: if Y married X or X married Y, then X is married to Y:

```
X is_married_to Y          :- Y married X ; X married Y.
```

The next rule will define parenthood by saying that if Y is X's child, then X is Y's parent:

```
X is_a_parent_of Y         :- Y is_a_child_of X.
```

Now we get specific about roles; you are a father if you are a parent and are male, and a mother if you are a parent and are female:

```
X is_the_father_of Y       :- X is_a_parent_of Y,
                              X is_male.
X is_the_mother_of Y       :- X is_a_parent_of Y,
                              X is_female.
```

We can do the same thing with sons and daughters:

```
X is_a_son_of Y              :- X is_a_child_of Y,
                                X is_male.
X is_a_daughter_of Y         :- X is_a_child_of Y,
                                X is_female.
```

Finally, let's take a look at how one defines brotherhood and sisterhood. First, we must identify the generic relationship of being siblings by indicating that two people are siblings if they have the same mother and the same father:

```
X is_a_sibling_of Y          :- Z is_the_mother_of Y,
                                Z is_the_mother_of X,
                                X is_the_father_of Y,
                                X is_the_father_of X,
                                X \= Y.
```

The last line, **X** $\setminus$ = **Y**, indicates that you cannot be the sibling to yourself. The reason for this seemingly strange piece of code is to prevent Prolog from coming to that conclusion when it "plugs" the same value into two different variables which it will eventually do in its exhaustive search to fulfill a goal.

Now we can declare brotherhood and sisterhood as the state of being one's sibling and being of the appropriate sex:

```
X is_a_brother_of Y          :- X is_a_sibling_of Y,
                                X is_male.
X is_a_sister_of Y           :- X is_a_sibling_of Y,
                                X is_female.
```

Remember that the whole code has not been presented here, some of the typical queries that we could make would be as follows:

```
relation(pamela,rachel).
    pamela is rachel's mother.
    rachel is pamela's daughter.

X is_a_son_of edgar.
    X=george ;
    X=irving ;
    X=jeff ;
    no.
```

```
A is_a_niece_of B.
   A=odette, B=heather ;
   A=odette, B=irving ;
   A=odette, B=pamela ;
   A=odette, B=jeff  ;
   A=odette, B=karen ;
   A=rachel, B=george ;
   A=rachel, B=linda ;
   A=rachel, B=heather ;
   A=rachel, B=jeff ;
   A=rachel, B=irving ;
   A=tina, B=george ;
   A=tina, B=linda ;
   A=tina, B=heather ;
   A=tina, B=irving ;
   A=tina, B=pamela ;
   A=tina, B=jeff ;
   no.
```

Such is a simple consultation with Prolog.

SUMMARY

There are two types of AI languages available in the mainstream of AI work: list processing languages, like LISP and Pop-11, and logic programming languages, like Prolog. List processing languages offer strengths in processing words, sentences, and so forth in a manner that encourages rapid prototyping and easy testing. These languages give the user a great deal of control over the inner workings of the program but require a corresponding effort to keep things running smoothly.

Prolog is better suited to situations in which the knowledge to be processed consists of facts and relationships between these facts. It offers an easier method of programming, in the broad sense, but as a result makes it more difficult for the user to exert any detailed control over the operation of the system.

The question of which language is best to use for AI is really a function of the type of application being developed. Expert systems, natural language systems, and so on will lend themselves nicely to Prolog, whereas most other applications will find a friend in either LISP or Pop-11. Some efforts have been made at bringing out a hybrid language, most notably the language LogLisp, a product of Syracuse University.

Both types of languages have difficulty with numeric processing, owing to the large amounts of overhead that they require for all their "bells and whistles." Companies that choose this route have made a serious commitment, not only to AI but to research and development in AI, since the systems developed here are too expensive to be used for a one-shot application.

One solution to this problem has been to build special-purpose machines, but the cost per user for these machines is quite high. One system that attempts to combine a solution for the problem of which language to use along with the problem of numeric processing is Poplog, originally developed at the University of Sussex. This system allows the three languages—Pop-11, Prolog, and LISP—to be mixed together in the same program. It also allows traditional languages to be brought into the AI system so that their numeric processing abilities may be fully utilized.

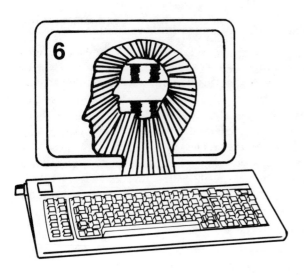

Problem Solving

The question of how to solve problems is perhaps one of the most germane to the overall task of creating systems with artificial intelligence techniques. After all, it is the way in which we solve problems that has the most practical application to the question of how people think: it is, in fact, the reason that we try to bring these principles to a computer system. If the system that we develop solves problems in a manner that somehow approximates that manner in which people solve problems, then (hopefully) the system will be able to take advantage of the methods that people use and thereby become more accurate, more efficient, or more creative.

Much of the efforts spent on bringing human problem-solving techniques to computer systems has been in the realm of solving what might be termed *classic* problems, or puzzles. The game of chess, for example, has presented a long-standing challenge not only to computers but to mechanical systems in general; chess can rightly be viewed as a puzzle, albeit a highly complex one. Some of the other classic problems studied by AI researchers at first glance appear more mundane, but these also represent serious challenges to the computer; these include the oriental game of Go, the game of checkers, the Traveling Salesman problem, the 15-square puzzle, and many others. We will examine these challenges in an overview and then present two of them as programming exercises, each of which will take advantage of the dynamic memory system in BASIC.

One of the "metaproblems" to be addressed during the pursuit of problem-solving is that of how to generalize some sense of the human problem-solving process out of the collection of specific problem-solving strategies that are assembled. As the reader will see from the approaches to solving the problems that follow, there is nothing in any one of the approaches that seems to capture this generalized sense of human problem solving; instead, there is perhaps the notion that some person has been involved in the process, but nothing particularly "human" has arisen as a result. This is, perhaps, one of the reasons for the "old" saying about artificial intelligence applications: "If you can do it with a computer, the problem never actually required AI to begin with!"

CHESS

Most people are familiar with the game of chess, but a brief review for the purposes of seeing how it might be approached in AI is in order: in chess, there are two players, Black and White, each of whom has 16 pieces. The game is played on a board that is 8 squares wide (rows) and 8 squares long (columns). Each player begins the game by lining up their pieces on the two rows nearest them. There are six types of pieces, with the following characteristics:

Pawn: moves one square forward (towards the other player); it captures an opposing piece when that piece is on a square that is diagonally in front of it; it may move two squares forward on its first move *only*. Each player has eight pawns.

Rook: moves in any direction orthogonally (that is, on the rows and columns, *not* diagonally), as many squares as desired. Each player has two rooks.

Knight: moves one square orthogonally, then one square diagonally, in any direction. It is not "blocked" by another piece or pieces in its way. Each player has two knights.

Bishop: moves in any direction diagonally, as many squares as desired. Each player has two bishops.

Queen: moves in any direction, orthogonally or diagonally, as many squares as desired. Each player has one queen.

King: moves one square only in any direction, orthogonally or diagonally, with the exception of castling (described later). Each player has one king.

When a piece is moved, it may be moved up to its limit, providing there is no other piece, whether "friendly" or not, in its path. If there is an "unfriendly" piece in its path, the piece must either capture it (and in doing so, remove it from the game), or stop before reaching the opposing piece. Exceptions are castling (described later) and knights.

Play alternates between the two players, each player moving one piece per turn, with the exception of castling (described later).

The white player moves first.

When one player can capture the other's king on the next move, and the other player cannot avoid having their king captured, the first player wins the game (*checkmate*).

You can see how the rules are built up, with a series of exceptions arising along the way. None of these rules explicitly contain any strategies, or metarules; these must be derived in some alternative fashion.

Thinking about the way the game is organized for a moment, you could view the game as a tree, with the "pristine" board at the root. There are 20 possible first moves (white), so the first level of the tree would contain 20 nodes. There are 20 second moves (black's first move), so that each node at the first level would have 20 children at the second level, or 400 (20 × 20) altogether. If there were 20 third moves (white's second move)—but there are more!—there would be 8,000 (20 × 40) at the third level, and so on. Clearly there is a problem with exponential expansion here, and some heuristics must be used.

One classical method of assessing the game is to assign point values to each of the pieces: pawn = 1, rook = 5, knight = 2.5, bishop = 3, and queen = 10. Using this strategy alone, one could "look ahead" a few moves (most human chess masters look in the neighborhood of 10 moves ahead), and pick the move with the best mini-max score (my total minus yours). This strategy, however, would ignore the advantages of position that have been clearly laid out, such as the four central squares being of critical importance to control throughout the beginning and middle of the game. Also, to represent the problem of checkmate, you would have to assign a large point value to the king, say perhaps 10,000. In addition, some scoring conventions assign a larger value to the knight as long as the opposing queen is on the board, so again, the effectiveness of this approach would probably have to be assessed.

Even so, this manner of playing the game does not really match that of a human chess player. The typical chess master, though they may look many moves in advance, does not look at *every* possible combination of moves; indeed, what seems part and parcel of their expertise is the ability *not to notice* moves that are either nonproductive or bad. Clearly they focus their attention—in ways they cannot describe—on sequences of moves that are "most likely" to be productive or dangerous.

GO

The rules of chess are fairly easy to state, but they are immensely complicated when compared with the oriental game of Go. And yet Go is much more difficult to program than chess, in terms of producing a program that has any hope of playing a good game. A brief look at Go will illustrate why.

Go is another two-player game in which players taking black or white pieces. It is played on a 19 × 19 board, and there is only one type of piece, a simple marker. Once a piece is placed on the board, it cannot be moved to a new location on the board; it may, however, be captured and removed from the board.

A piece is considered "alive" if:

1. it is orthagonally adjacent to an empty location; or
2. it is orthagonally adjacent to a friendly piece that is alive.

If a piece is not alive, it is captured and removed from play. A player's turn consists of putting one piece somewhere on the board. Play alternates between the two players, with Black moving first. A piece may not be played if it would be "dead" at the end of your move.

The winner is the person who, after no new moves can be made, has the greatest score. The score is figured by subtracting the number of pieces a player has lost from the number of locations that he or she controls on the board; that is, the spaces that are occupied or surrounded by his or her pieces.

That is the essence of the game. There is one last rule used for resolving circular captures that is equally simple, but beyond the scope of this discussion.

Why then is Go so difficult to program?

First of all, recall the size of the board: there are 19 × 19, or 361 locations available for play. Pieces are not likely to be captured in the first 20 moves or so, so that the twentieth level of the game tree would have approximately 4×10^{32} nodes! This compares with about 10^{26} nodes at the twentieth level for chess: there are more than 4 million times more moves for Go! What makes this even more complicated is that, unlike chess, a move very early in the game (say, a player's fourth or fifth move) can be recognized by experts as good or bad, even though the effect of that move will not be felt until perhaps 40 or 50 moves—or even more—have transpired. There is a distinct sense that Go masters have of the "feel" of the entire board, which may be different depending on which location a player moves to—and the occupation of adjacent locations may make the board "feel" very different, even early in the game, when the board is sparsely populated.

CHECKERS

Checkers is an example of a game that has been explored as an AI problem from the earliest days of the field. In 1959 Dr. A. Samuels decided to create a program to play an "intelligent" game of checkers, and the system he developed has since become known as the "Samuels Checkers Player." He attempted, with some success, to develop a program that would not simply play a good game of checkers, but would somehow simulate the learning process. He therefore approached a number of expert checkers players and obtained records of the games that they had played. He then fed each of these games into his program, building a knowledge base of every move in every game. He then created two computer programs to play each other, and recorded all of their games as well.

Each program learned from both the experience of the human players and the games it played with the other program, in the sense that it derived a scoring function from the wealth of games that had been recorded, and applied that scoring function to a MiniMax search of the game it was currently playing. All in all, the program stored over 53,000 games in an attempt to play the best game possible.

The Samuels Checkers Player never became a serious contender in the Checkers field, for a combination of reasons; a lack of an adequate scoring function was certainly central. However the problem of storing and traversing the massive amounts of data required for storing 53,000 games, particularly with the computer hardware technology that was available in the early 1960's, was a significant one. It is to Samuel's credit that his program played a respectable game of checkers at all, and the developments he pioneered in his efforts led to some of the more useful algorithms in AI, such as the Alpha-Beta Pruning procedure.

Let us explore two classic AI problems: that of the Traveling Salesman and that of the Tiles problem. Each of these problems will be followed by a BASIC program you can try.

THE TRAVELING SALESMAN PROBLEM

The Traveling Salesman problem is a classic in the field of artificial intelligence, and one that has many practical applications in the business world. The object is to find the shortest route or circuit that "visits" each of a series of points exactly once. This problem has not been proven to be "solvable" in mathematical terms, but it—and its "cousins"—must be solved to some degree every day in the working world of scheduling, and routing.

The AI approach to this problem illustrates the difficulties inherent in solutions by *total enumeration* or by the examination of all alternatives. It also serves to clarify that AI, while producing "intelligent" solutions, does not lay claim to mathematically perfect ones.

Simply stated, the problem can be described as follows: given a number of cities (or nodes on a graph) and the distance between them (values that are placed on the arcs between the nodes), find a route that will start at any city, visit each city once and only once, and end at the starting city, thus forming a circuit. Furthermore, the route chosen should be the shortest one possible; that is, the sum of the arcs used to visit each node should be the smallest sum possible.

The applications to the working world are many: planning actual sales routes, delivery routes, transportation routes, and so on; and plotting the best *critical path* through a complicated planning graph. The list of applications can be as diverse as desired.

For a small number of cities, the problem is trivial. Presuming that the cost of traveling between two cities is the same, no matter which direction is chosen, if there are four cities, there are at most six routes that can be used between cities:

Let us label the four cities A, B, C, and D. Let us further suppose that each of the four cities has routes to all the others available to it. We may then represent each of the possible routes by a list of the cities in the order that we visited them. One of the possible routes, then, will be "ABCD": we start at city A, visit B next, then C, then D, and finally return to A. By taking all the permutations of the letters, with A as the first (arbitrarily), we can generate all the possible routes, which are:

1. ABCD
2. ABDC
3. ACBD
4. ACDB
5. ADBC
6. ADCB

Note that if we had taken B as the first city, we would have arrived at the same list of routes, just in a different sequence. For example, taking B as the first city, we would have generated the following sequence of routes, which are referenced to the list above:

4. BACD
6. BADC
5. BCAD
1. BCDA
3. BDAC
2. BDCA

The reason that this holds true is a mathematical issue that is beyond the scope of this chapter.

Now it would not be any terrific feat to examine each of these six routes and find the shortest one. The number of possible routes, however, increases geometrically as the number of cities increases, which means that the number of routes gets very large very quickly. The specific formula is:

$$(n-1)!$$

where n is the number of cities, and ! refers to the factorial function. Thus, while four cities have 6 routes, five have 24, six have 120, and so on. The number of routes between each of the fifty capitals is (49)!, or approximately $6.08 * 10^{62}$: a number that starts with 6 and is followed by 62 zeroes! If a computer examined a million routes every second, it would have to work

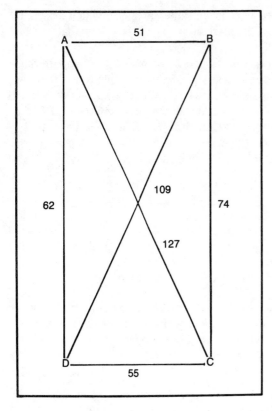

Fig. 6-1. A map of four cities.

for $1.93 * 10^{49}$ years before it examined every one; such a task is obviously not reasonable.

The two brute force methods of solving this problem, *depth first* and *breadth first* search, will fail due to the enormity of the numbers of options that must be considered. It is, however, worth examining how they might be applied to such a task. We can create a *tree* of solutions, by generating a tree of possible routes from each point. It will, in fact, be the method of generating this tree that illustrates the notion of depth or breadth first search.

Let us use the simple problem of four cities, and examine a depth first strategy to begin with. First, we will need a map of the four cities, as shown in Fig. 6-1.

Let us presume that *next* will be defined as *clockwise* for the purposes of this example.

The depth-first strategy is to take the first child available, place it on the tree, and then find *its* first child, and so on, until a complete route is generated. Then one "backs up" a level, generates the next child, and on and on, until the entire tree is filled. Tree 1 in Fig. 6-2 shows how this would look after one complete route:

Next we would add the first alternate route that we could generate, which would be from point B, as shown in Tree 2 in Fig. 6-2.

This represents all the possible alternatives for B having started at A, so we would next generate the other alternatives to B. Taking C as the next alternative, we would generate Tree 3 in Fig. 6-2.

And finally, the routes from the alternative D can be added, as shown in Tree 4 in Fig. 6-2.

You may notice that there are only three different distances given above, when there are supposedly six different routes. The reason for this is that we are considering the *order* in which a route is traveled to be significant; that is, it might take longer to get from Albany to New York than to get from New York to Albany (given traffic flow, for example).

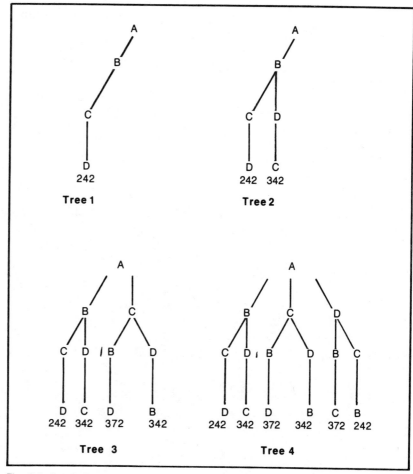

Fig. 6-2. Depth first trees used to evaluate different possible routes.

Artificial Intelligence: Theory, Logic and Application

The "dumb" way to utilize this method would be to construct the complete tree and then find the route with the smallest distance. A smarter way would be to take the total of the first route, save it as the "lowest distance to date," and then compare it with each segment as it is generated. The advantage of taking this smarter alternative is that whole branches of the tree could be avoided when they could be proved to be "obviously" unprofitable.

Now, the breadth-first approach generates the same tree, but in a different manner, which turns out to be even less suitable: first one finds all the possible routes starting at A, and generates a two-level tree, such as Tree 1 in Fig. 6-3.

Next, one generates the next set of alternatives, producing the third level of the tree, as shown in Tree 2 in Fig. 6-3.

Finally, the fourth level is generated, producing the same tree as before, shown in Tree 3 in Fig. 6-3.

The disadvantage to this method is that interim results cannot be compared to a "best try," and as such the entire tree must be generated. Thus, this method will have no practical application to this problem.

How can this problem be solved in a reasonable manner? One approach that appears to work quite well and can generate the best route within any desired probability, uses an intuitive method that has been translated into an algorithm or computer program.

The conceptual strategy revolves around the notion that the best route will bear some resemblance to a circle: the route will not criss-cross from one city to another, but skirt around the edge of the group as much as possi-

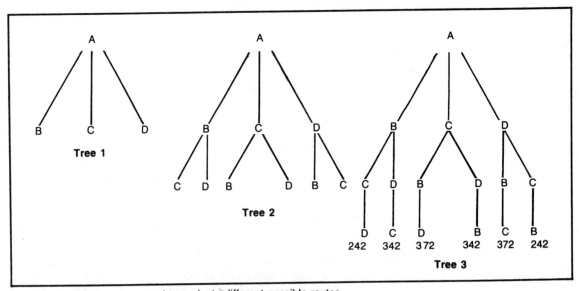

Fig. 6-3. Breadth first trees used to evaluate different possible routes.

ble. With this metagoal in mind, it is possible to devise an algorithm that sets up a first try at such a route and then refines it to within a desired tolerance:

Remember that the following algorithm gives only a *good* solution, not a guaranteed *best* solution:

1. Choose a city as the starting city, either by definition or at random.

2. Find the city farthest from the start city, and establish a link between the two.

3. Find the city farthest from the city in step 2, and link it to both that city and the first, creating a closed loop. This third city is the "most recent" city.

LOOP   4. If there are no cities left, go to TEST.

5. Locate the city furthest from the "most recent" city. Label this city the "most recent" city.

6. Find the two cities closest to the "most recent" city. Insert the "most recent" city in the route between them.

7. Go to LOOP.

TEST   8. Set TEST_NUMBER = 0. Set BEST_DISTANCE = length of route.

LOOP1   9. Add 1 to TEST_NUMBER.

10. If TEST_NUMBER = some maximum number, go to EXIT.

11. Choose three routes at random, designated as $\overline{IJ}, \overline{KL}, \overline{MN}$, where the letters I - N indicate cities.

12. Temporarily replace these routes with $\overline{IL}, \overline{KN}, \overline{MJ}$.

13. Recompute the length of the circuit. If it is greater than or equal to the value of BEST_DISTANCE, then restore the original routes and go to LOOP1.

14. A better route has been found. Make the replacements permanent and go to TEST.

EXIT   15. Output the route and BEST_DISTANCE, then finish.

This procedure will calculate the shortest route within the tolerance specified in step 10: if the distance had to be the best to a factor of 1/100 then the maximum number of tests to compare TEST_NUMBER against would be 100; for 1/1,000 the maximum number would be 1,000. Of course, the greater the desired accuracy, the longer the TEST loop will take, but this is not the incredible expansion that erupts if one were to try to generate all possible routes.

Notice that there is nothing about this program that implies that the computer is smart or clever; such attributes may well be given to the originators of this algorithm, but certainly there is nothing amazing about the program that is generated from this algorithm.

Further refinements to the performance of the program designed to solve this problem can be made: one would be to store the distances between cities in a table, only calculating them once. For fifty cities, there will be 1,225 distances to compute if distances are equal in both directions (2,450 otherwise); by precalculating and then doing simple lookups, the run time of the program can be dramatically improved.

As an exercise, what form of data structure would best be used to solve this problem? Recall that we will be generating a route, or list of cities, and that these cities will be a certain distance from each other. We will want to be able to traverse this route, totalling the distance as we go.

Another thing that we will want to be able to do with this list is to remove segments of it (during the test phase) and replace them with others. For

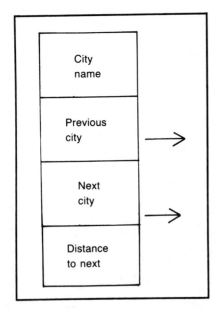

Fig. 6-4. A doubly linked data structure.

this purpose, it would seem to be a good idea to be able to determine which city lay before a given city, as well as after it.

In data structure terminology, this means we need a *doubly-linked list*, or one that provides backward and forward pointers at each node. Thus, we might represent this structure as shown in Fig. 6-4.

If you use the shell provided for BASIC processing, you will probably want to code the city names with a single integer to save in processing time. You will also want to round off distances to the nearest integer, again to save complications.

The Traveling Salesman Problem Program

```
1000 ' ***************************
1010 ' *                         *
1020 ' *      Traveling Salesman  *
1030 ' *         Problem          *
1040 ' *                         *
1050 ' *                         *
1060 ' * Artificial Intelligence: *
1070 ' *                         *
1080 ' *      Theory, Logic       *
1090 ' *      and Application     *
1100 ' *                         *
1110 ' *                         *
1120 ' *      James F. Brule'     *
1130 ' *                         *
1140 ' *         (c) 1985         *
1150 ' *                         *
1160 ' *                         *
1170 ' ***************************
1180 '
1190 ' **************
1200 ' * Initialize *
1210 ' **************
1220 '
1230 MAXMEM=3500
1240 P$="\                        \  #,###.##"
1250 Q$="-------------------------- ----------"
1260 R$="              TOTAL:    ##,###.##"
1270 '
1280 ' FNL = additional distance resulting from inserting
1290 '       node A between nodes X and Y
1300 '
```

```
1310 DEF FNL(A,X,Y) = ARCS(X,A)+ARCS(A,Y) - ARCS(X,Y)
1320 '
1330 ' FNR = random integer between 1 and 51
1340 '
1350 DEF FNR = INT(RND*51+1)
1360 '
1370 '
1380 DIM ARCS(51,51),STATE$(51),L(51,2),S%(MAXMEM)
1390 '
1400 ' input data
1410 '
1420 OPEN "I",#1,"B:TRAVEL.DAT"
1430 FOR I=1 TO 51
1440    INPUT#1, STATE$(I),L(I,1),L(I,2)
1450    ARCS(0,I)=0
1460    NEXT I
1470 CLOSE
1480 '
1490 ' translate geographic coordinates to distances
1500 '
1510 FOR I=1 TO 51
1520    FOR J=1 TO 51
1530      IF I=J THEN 1590
1540      IF I>J THEN 1570
1550      ARCS(I,J)=SQR(((L(I,1)-L(J,1))*50)^2 + ((L(I,2)-L(J,2))*70)
           ^2)
1560      GOTO 1600
1570      ARCS(I,J)=ARCS(J,I)
1580      GOTO 1600
1590      ARCS(I,J)=0
1600      NEXT J
1610    PRINT STATE$(I)
1620    NEXT I
1630 '
1640 ' constants
1650 '
1660 SIZE=0      :PTR=1       :N1=2       :N2=3
1670 TRUE=(1=1)  :FALSE=(1=0) :NIL=-1     :NEED=4
1680 FREEHD=0
1690 '
1700 ' setup dynamic memory
1710 '
1720 S%(0)=0:S%(1)=3:S%(3)=MAXMEM-6:S%(4)=MAXMEM-1
1730 S%(MAXMEM-1)=0:S%(MAXMEM)=NIL
```

```
1740 '
1750 RANDOMIZE
1760 '
1770 'setup IOBYTE
1780 '
1790 INPUT "[C]onsole or [P]rinter";CON$
1800 IF CON$<>"P" THEN 1850
1810 ON ERROR GOTO 1830
1820 POKE 3,130:GOTO 1850
1830 POKE 3,128
1840 PRINT "ERROR ENCOUNTERED":STOP
1850 '
1860 ' ***********************
1870 ' * Make Initial Circuit *
1880 ' ***********************
1890 '
1900 ' Set up a loop consisting of three arcs.
1910 ' Nodes are in linked loop.
1920 '
1930 GOSUB 2590:' gosub GETSTORE
1940 TOP=GLOC
1950 A=9:' start in the capitol, Washington DC
1960 ARCS(0,A)=1:' mark as used
1970 MAXIN=A
1980 GOSUB 3230:' gosub GETMAX
1990 B=MAX
2000 S%(TOP+N1)=A
2010 S%(TOP+N2)=B
2020 GOSUB 2590:' gosub GETSTORE
2030 TEMP=GLOC
2040 S%(TOP+PTR)=TEMP
2050 A=B
2060 MAXIN=A
2070 GOSUB 3230:' gosub GETMAX
2080 B=MAX
2090 S%(TEMP+N1)=A
2100 S%(TEMP+N2)=B
2110 GOSUB 2590:' gosub GETSTORE
2120 S%(TEMP+PTR)=GLOC
2130 TEMP=GLOC
2140 S%(TEMP+N1)=B
2150 S%(TEMP+N2)=S%(TOP+N1):' complete loop
2160 S%(TEMP+PTR)=TOP
2170 '
```

```
2180 ' *************
2190 ' * MAIN LOOP *
2200 ' *************
2210 '
2220 ' find furthest node from most recent addition
2230 '
2240 MAXIN=B
2250 GOSUB 3230:' gosub GETMAX
2260 A=MAX
2270 IF A=NIL THEN 2320:' all nodes processed
2280 GOSUB 3550:' gosub FINDSPOT
2290 B=A
2300 GOTO 2220
2310 '
2320 ' circuit complete; now test it
2330 '
2340 GOSUB 3870:' gosub TEST
2350 '
2360 ' job complete; now output results
2370 '
2380 TEMP=TOP
2390 '
2400 ' minor loop
2410 '
2420 DX=ARCS(S%(TEMP+N1),S%(TEMP+N2))
2430 PRINT USING P$; STATE$(S%(TEMP+N1)),DX
2440 CIRLEN=CIRLEN+DX
2450 TEMP=S%(TEMP+PTR)
2460 IF S%(TEMP+PTR)<>TOP THEN 2400
2470 '
2480 ' else print totals
2490 '
2500 PRINT Q$
2510 PRINT USING R$; CIRLEN
2520 PRINT CHR$(12):POKE 3,128:END
2530 '
2540 ' ************************
2550 ' * Subroutines Begin Here *
2560 ' ************************
2570 '
2580 '
2590 ' ************
2600 ' * getstore *
2610 ' ************
```

```
2620 '
2630 ' space required = NEED (hardcoded=4)
2640 ' index to block = GLOC
2650 '
2660 GTMP=FREEHD
2670 IF S%(GTMP+SIZE) >= NEED THEN 2750
2680 GTMP=S%(GTMP+PTR)
2690 IF GTMP <> NIL THEN 2670
2700 '
2710 ' no memory left: abort program
2720 '
2730 PRINT:PRINT "OUT OF MEMORY!":STOP
2740 '
2750 ' successful search
2760 '
2770 GLOC=GTMP+S%(GTMP+SIZE)-NEED
2780 S%(GLOC+SIZE)=NEED
2790 S%(GTMP+SIZE)=S%(GTMP+SIZE)-NEED
2800 RETURN
2810 '
2820 '
2830 ' ***********
2840 ' * putback *
2850 ' ***********
2860 '
2870 ' index to block = PLOC
2880 '
2890 PTMP=0
2900 IF S%(PTMP+PTR) > PLOC THEN 2940
2910 PTMP=S%(PTMP+PTR)
2920 GOTO 2900
2930 '
2940 ' place to insert found
2950 '
2960 S%(PLOC+PTR)=S%(PTMP+PTR)
2970 S%(PTMP+PTR)=PLOC
2980 '
2990 ' check for congruity
3000 '
3010 SQTOP=PLOC
3020 SQBOT=S%PLOC+PTR)
3030 GOSUB 3100:' gosub SQUASH
3040 SQTOP=PTMP
3050 SQBOT=PLOC
```

```
3060 GOSUB 3100:' gosub SQUASH
3070 RETURN
3080 '
3090 '
3100 ' **********
3110 ' * squash *
3120 ' **********
3130 '
3140 ' join two blocks if congruent
3150 ' smaller index = SQTOP; larger = SQBOT
3160 '
3170 IF (S%(SQTOP+SIZE)+SQTOP) <> SQBOT THEN RETURN
3180 S%(SQTOP+PTR)=S%(SQBOT+PTR)
3190 S%(SQTOP+SIZE)=S%(SQTOP+SIZE)+S%(SQBOT+SIZE)
3200 RETURN
3210 '
3220 '
3230 ' **********
3240 ' * getmax *
3250 ' **********
3260 '
3270 ' find node MAX, where MAX is furthest from MAXIN.
3280 ' search only unlcaimed nodes;
3290 ' update ARCS when through.
3300 ' return MAX=NIL if all nodes searched.
3310 '
3320 MAX=0
3330 FOR COL%=1 TO 51
3340    IF ARCS(0,COL%)=1 THEN 3360
3350    IF ARCS(MAXIN,COL%) > ARCS(MAXIN,MAX) THEN MAX=COL%
3360    NEXT COL%
3370 IF MAX=0 THEN MAX=NIL:RETURN:' all nodes searched
3380 ARCS(0,MAX)=1
3390 RETURN
3400 '
3410 '
3420 ' ***********
3430 ' * findrec *
3440 ' ***********
3450 '
3460 ' FPTR = starting loc; L = current index; T = goal
3470 ' Find Tth record in linked list
3480 '
3490 IF L=T THEN RETURN
```

```
3500 L=L+1
3510 FPTR=S%(FPTR+PTR)
3520 GOTO 3490
3530 '
3540 '
3550 ' ************
3560 ' * findspot *
3570 ' ************
3580 '
3590 ' insert node A in circuit,
3600 ' minimizing increase in distance.
3610 '
3620 GOSUB 2590:' gosub GETSTORE
3630 S%(GLOC+N1)=A
3640 BEST=FNL(A,S%(TOP+N1),S%(TOP+N2))
3650 TEMP=TOP
3660 '
3670 ' loop
3680 '
3690 TEMP=S%(TEMP+PTR)
3700 IF FNL(A,S%(TEMP+N1),S%(TEMP+N2)) >= BEST THEN 3740
3710 BEST=FNL(A,S%(TEMP+N1),S%(TEMP+N2))
3720 BESTREC=TEMP
3730 '
3740 ' test to see if done
3750 '
3760 IF S%(TEMP+PTR) <> TOP THEN 3670
3770 '
3780 ' best arcs found; insert new node in circuit
3790 '
3800 S%(GLOC+N2)=S%(BESTREC+N2)
3810 S%(GLOC+PTR)=S%(BESTREC+PTR)
3820 S%(BESTREC+N2)=A
3830 S%(BESTREC+PTR)=GLOC
3840 RETURN
3850 '
3860 '
3870 ' ********
3880 ' * test *
3890 ' ********
3900 '
3910 ' Attempt 100 alternative circuits
3920 ' if any are shorter, replace and restart TEST
3930 '
```

```
3940 TEST=1
3950 '
3960 ' generate 3 arcs for testing
3970 '
3980 T1=FNR
3990 T2=FNR:IF T2=T1 THEN 3990
4000 T3=FNR:IF (T1=T3) OR (T2=T3) THEN 4000
4010 '
4020 ' sort
4030 '
4040 IF T3<T2 THEN SWAP T3,T2
4050 IF T2<T1 THEN SWAP T2,T1
4060 IF T3<T2 THEN SWAP T3,T2
4070 '
4080 ' locate
4090 '
4100 FPTR=TOP
4110 L=1
4120 T=T1
4130 GOSUB 3420:'gosub FINDREC
4140 I1=S%(FPTR+N1):I2=S%(FPTR+N2):IPTR=FPTR
4150 T=T2
4160 GOSUB 3420:'gosub FINDREC
4170 J1=S%(FPTR+N1):J2=S%(FPTR+N2):JPTR=FPTR
4180 T=T3
4190 GOSUB 3420:' gosub FINDREC
4200 K1=S%(FPTR+N1):K2=S%(FPTR+N2):KPTR=FPTR
4210 '
4220 ' Three nodes found: check distances
4230 '
4240 TOT1=ARCS(I1,I2)+ARCS(J1,J2)+ARCS(K1,K2)
4250 TOT2=ARCS(I1,J2)+ARCS(J1,K2)+ARCS(K1,I2)
4260 IF TOT2 < TOT1 THEN 4370
4270 '
4280 ' no improvement found
4290 '
4300 TEST=TEST+1
4310 IF TEST < 100 THEN 3960
4320 '
4330 ' else
4340 '
4350 RETURN
4360 '
4370 ' Shorter route found
```

```
4380 '
4390 PRINT "Shorter route found: restarting"
4400 S%(IPTR+N2)=J2
4410 S%(JPTR+N2)=K2
4420 S%(KPTR+N2)=I2
4430 TEST=1
4440 GOTO 3960
```

<u>Traveling Salesman Data: TRAVEL.DAT</u>

```
Alabama,32,86
Alaska,58,134
Arizona,33,112
Arkansas,35,92
California,38,121
Colorado,40,105
Connecticut,42,73
Delaware,39,76
District of Columbia,39.5,77
Florida,30,84
Georgia,34,84
Hawaii,21,158
Idaho,44,116
Illinois,40,90
Indiana,40,86
Iowa,41,94
Kansas,39,96
Kentucky,38,85
Louisiana,30,91
Maine,44,70
Maryland,39,77
Massachusetts,42,71
Michigan,43,85
Minnesota,43,95
Mississippi,32,90
Missouri,39,92
Montana,47,112
Nebraska,41,97
Nevada,39,119
New Hampshire,43,72
New Jersey,40,75
New Mexico,36,106
New York,43,74
```

```
North Carolina,36,79
North Dakota,47,101
Ohio,40,83
Oklahoma,35,98
Oregon,45,123
Pennsylvania,40,77
Rhode Island,42,71
South Carolina,34,81
South Dakota,44,100
Tennessee,36,87
Texas,30,97
Utah,41,112
Vermont,44,73
Virginia,38,77
Washington,47,123
West Virginia,38,82
Wisconson,43,89
Wyoming,41,105
```

THE TILES PROBLEM

Almost everyone has played with the puzzle in which a number of tiles are scrambled up in a horizontal case, and by shifting them past each other one at a time, the person tries to rearrange them in the proper order. One method of solving this kind of problem requires the use of backtracking, or reversing decisions as they are discovered to be unproductive. In this case, however, we will explore a method that will be more efficient than simply generating all possible moves and moving around until we stumble on the correct one.

In the programming example given, we will use a board that is 3 × 3, filled with eight tiles (one space is left blank). Furthermore, in defining the "moves" of the puzzle, we will talk about moving the space up, down, right, or left, rather than worrying about which tile can move into the space. A little thought will clarify that these two approaches will result in the same puzzle; the former just happens to be easier to work with.

As we try to move the puzzle around towards the solution, we can imagine that we are generating a graph and exploring it by visiting a node, generating its children, visiting the most likely candidate out of *all* the children so far, and continuing on until the puzzle is completed. This procedure is known as the *A ∗ algorithm*, developed by Nilsson.

In order to accomplish this, we will need to have a method of telling which child is the most likely candidate; in other words, we need a *heuristic*. In fact, we will use one of a combination of four heuristics, scoring each possible child according to each of these approaches. The heuristics we will use will be:

1. The total number of tiles in the correct position. This score is *added* to the score for each node.
2. The total *Manhattan distance* of all the tiles. This is calculated by adding the number of rows and columns that each tile is out of position. This score is *subtracted* from the score for each node.
3. The sequence: This is basically a count of how many correct neighbors each node has. This is a positive score and as such is added to the total.
4. The modularity: If an even numbered piece is in an even numbered spot, then that is a positive score.

Each child, as it is generated, has a score attached to it. All the children are then arranged in order of their scores and linked together through the use of pointers. The child with the best score is explored next, after which it is removed from the list of unexplored nodes, and its children are inserted into the list in the proper order (given their scores).

All the while that this is going on, another set of links are being maintained to keep track of the route that will be followed once the solution is found.

This represents a more advanced programming example, and as such most readers will want to leave it for a later date to explore in detail. If you would like to try "fiddling" with the program, however, here are some of the parts of it that you may want to explore.

First of all, this is a program that uses the dynamic memory scheme outlined in Chapter 4. The memory management routines begin at line 12000.

Each child is built up as a frame, where each frame contains the following information: a pointer to the next unexplored node, a measure of how deep into the tree the child is, what the child's parent (**DAD**) is, what move was used to generate the child from its parent, what position the tiles are in, what the score for the child is, and whether or not it has been explored. Also included is a hashing number, so that children can be stored and retrieved more quickly. These qualities are outlined beginning at line 10480.

Beginning at line 18000 are the heuristic *flags* P1-P4. When these variables are set to +1, the value of that particular heuristic is *added* to the child's score; if it is −1, the value is *subtracted*, and if it is 0, the value is disregarded altogether. Try experimenting with different values and see what impact that has on the ease of solution.

The other area in which to experiment is in the data file `STARTST.DAT`, which defines the starting state of the puzzle. Try different beginning states and see how well the program handles them.

Finally, the last four lines of the program are specific to the CP/M operating system, and are used to toggle the printer on and off. If you are using a different system, you will need to either replace these lines with a simple RETURN statement or substitute the appropriate codes for your operating system.

The Tiles Problem Program

```
10000 ' *****************************
10010 ' *                           *
10020 ' *     Eight Tile Problem    *
10030 ' *                           *
10040 ' *     Heuristic Approach    *
10050 ' *                           *
10060 ' *                           *
10070 ' *                           *
10080 ' * Artificial Intelligence:  *
10090 ' *                           *
10100 ' *     Theory, Logic and     *
10110 ' *                           *
10120 ' *        Application        *
10130 ' *                           *
10140 ' *            by             *
10150 ' *                           *
10160 ' *     James F. Brule'       *
10170 ' *         (c) 1985          *
10180 ' *                           *
10190 ' *****************************
10195 '
10200 INPUT "[C]onsole or [P]rinter";CON$
10210 IF CON$<>"P" THEN 10280
10220 ON ERROR GOTO 10250
10221 '
10222 ' Set up easy access to printer:  ***CP/M dependant! ***
10223 '
10230 GOSUB 29060:' Change Console to Printer
10240 GOTO 10280
10250 GOSUB 29040:' Change Printer to Console
10251 '
10252 ' Install generic error trapping
10253 '
10260 PRINT "ERROR ENCOUNTERED":STOP
10270 '
10271 '
```

```
10272 ' Main program begins here:
10273 '
10274 '
10280 DEFINT A-Q,S-Z
10281 '
10282 ' Function Definitions
10283 '
10284 '
10290 DEF FNX(L)=((L-1) MOD 3) + 1
10291 '
10300 DEF FNY(L)=INT((L+2) / 3)
10301 '
10302 ' Debugging message:
10303 '
10310 PRINT "begin*";
10311 '
10312 ' Create labels for moves
10320 DIM M$(4):RESTORE 10340
10330 FOR I=1 TO 4:READ M$(I):NEXT I
10340 DATA Up,Right,Down,Left
10341 '
10350 MAXMEM=7500
10360 DIM S(MAXMEM)
10361 '
10362 ' Golden Mean - for use in hashing algorithm
10363 '
10370 RGM=.612542
10371 '
10372 ' Switches for Heuristics
10373 '
10380 A1=1:A2=-1:A3=1:A4=1:AL=-1:' see HEURISTIC
10381 '
10382 ' Global definitions
10383 '
10390 TRUE=(1=1):FALSE=(1=0):NIL=-1
10391
10392 ' Read in initial state
10393
10400 RESTORE 10410:FOR I=1 TO 9:READ GOAL(I):NEXT I
10410 DATA 1,2,3,8,0,4,7,6,5
10411 '
10412 ' Cumulative ordering for "Sequence" heuristic
10413 '
10420 RESTORE 10430:FOR I=1 TO 9:READ SEQ(I):NEXT I
```

```
10430 DATA 1,1,3,3,-1,-1,-3,1,-4
10431 '
10440 ' **********************
10450 ' * Program Constants *
10460 ' **********************
10461 '
10462 ' Debugging message:
10463 '
10470 PRINT "constants*";
10471 '
10480 SIZE=0       :PTR=1          :LEVEL=2
10490 FATHER=3     :OPRTN=4        :STATE=4
10500 HEUR=14      :HASH=15        :EXPLRD=16
10510 ORGIDX=2     :FREEHD=0       :STKNEED=3
10520 LSTNEED=3    :NODENEED=17
10521 '
10530 ' **************
10540 ' * Initialize *
10550 ' **************
10551 '
10552 ' Debugging message:
10553 '
10560 PRINT "initializing*";
10570 S(0)=0:S(1)=3:S(3)=MAXMEM-6:S(4)=MAXMEM-1
10580 S(MAXMEM-1)=0:S(MAXMEM)=NIL
10590 NEED=LSTNEED
10600 GOSUB 14000:' gosub GETSTORE
10610 LEAFHD=GLOC:S(LEAFHD+PTR)=NIL
10620 GOSUB 14000:' gosub GETSTORE
10630 STKHD=GLOC:S(STKHD+PTR)=NIL
10640 NEED=NODENEED
10650 GOSUB 14000:' gosub GETSTORE
10660 GOALST=GLOC
10670 FOR I=1 TO 9
10680    S(GOALST+STATE+I)=GOAL(I)
10690    NEXT I
10700 NEED=NODENEED
10710 GOSUB 14000:' gosub GETSTORE
10720 STARTST=GLOC
10730 OPEN "I",#1,"B:STARTST.DAT"
10740 FOR I=1 TO 9
10750    INPUT#1, S(STARTST+STATE+I)
10760    NEXT I
10770 CLOSE
```

```
10780 PRINT:PRINT "STARTING STATE:"
10790 PNODE=STARTST
10800 GOSUB 27000
10810 GOSUB 17000:' gosub INITHASH
10820 S(STARTST+FATHER)=0
10830 S(STARTST+LEVEL)=0
10840 HNODE=STARTST
10850 GOSUB 20000:' gosub HASH
10860 S(STARTST+HASH)=HTOT
10870 CUR=STARTST
10880 QREC1=GOALST
10890 QREC2=CUR
10900 GOSUB 19000:' gosub EQSTATE
10910 IF EQSTATE=TRUE THEN 11270
11000 '
11010 ' ****************
11020 ' * MAIN PROGRAM *
11030 ' ****************
11040 DAD=CUR
11041 '
11042 ' Debugging message:
11043 '
11050 PRINT:PRINT "main loop*";
11060 FOR MOVE=1 TO 4
11070    MVNUM=MOVE
11080    GOSUB 23000:' gosub MAKEKID
11090    IF KID=NIL THEN 11180
11100    QREC1=GOALST
11110    QREC2=KID
11120    GOSUB 19000:' gosub EQSTATE
11130    IF EQSTATE=TRUE THEN 11270
11140    LNODE=KID
11150    GOSUB 26000:' gosub LINK_TO_LIST
11160    PNODE=KID
11170    GOSUB 27000:' gosub PRINTNODE
11180    NEXT MOVE
11190 S(DAD+EXPLRD)=TRUE
11200 CNODE=DAD
11210 GOSUB 21000:' gosub ADD2CLOSED
11220 CUR=S(LEAFHD+PTR)
11230 IF CUR=NIL THEN 11460:' out of leaf nodes
11240 LEAFHD=S(LEAFHD+PTR)
11250 GOSUB 28000:' gosub PRINT OPEN NODES
11260 GOTO 11000
```

```
11270 '
11280 ' ********************
11290 ' * Goal State Found *
11300 ' ********************
11310 PRINT:PRINT "GOAL STATE FOUND!"
11320 STKHD=NIL
11330 GOSUB 15000:' gosub PUSH
11340 IF S(KID+LEVEL)=0 THEN 11370
11350 KID=S(KID+FATHER)
11360 GOTO 11330
11370 PRINT:PRINT " ",,"Solution:"
11380 M=S(S(STKHD+ORGIDX)+OPRTN)
11390 IF M=0 THEN 11410:' drop first record
11400 PRINT " ",M$(M)
11410 GOSUB 16000:' gosub POP
11420 IF STKHD <> NIL THEN 11380
11430 ' Exit Gracefully
11440 PRINT " ","B-D B-D B-D That's All Folks!"
11450 GOSUB 29030:END
11460 ' No Leaf Nodes found
11470 PRINT "No leaf nodes found: ABEND..."
11480 GOSUB 29030:STOP
11490 '
11500 ' *************************
11510 ' * Subroutines Begin Here *
11520 ' *************************
12000 '
12001 '
12002 ' Debugging message:
12003 '
12010 PRINT "squash*";
12020 ' subroutine SQUASH
12030 ' join two blocks if congruent
12040 ' smaller index = SQTOP; larger = SQBOT
12050 IF (S(SQTOP+SIZE)+SQTOP) <> SQBOT THEN RETURN
12060 S(SQTOP+PTR)=S(SQBOT+PTR)
12070 S(SQTOP+SIZE)=S(SQTOP+SIZE)+S(SQBOT+SIZE)
12080 RETURN
13000 '
13001 '
13002 ' Debugging message:
13003 '
13010 PRINT "putback*";
13020 ' subroutine PUTBACK
```

```
13030 ' index to block = PLOC
13040 PTMP=0
13050 IF S(PTMP+PTR) > PLOC THEN 13080
13060 PTMP=S(PTMP+PTR)
13070 GOTO 13050
13080 ' place to insert found
13090 S(PLOC+PTR)=S(PTMP+PTR)
13100 S(PTMP+PTR)=PLOC
13110 ' check for congruity
13120 SQTOP=PLOC
13130 SQBOT=S(PLOC+PTR)
13140 GOSUB 12000:' gosub SQUASH
13150 SQTOP=PTMP
13160 SQBOT=PLOC
13170 GOSUB 12000:' gosub SQUASH
13180 RETURN
14000 '
14001 '
14002 ' Debugging message:
14003 '
14010 PRINT "getstore*";
10411 '
14020 ' subroutine GETSTORE
14030 ' space required = NEED
14040 ' index to block = GLOC
14050 GTMP=FREEHD
14060 IF S(GTMP+SIZE) >= NEED THEN 14230
14070 GTMP=S(GTMP+PTR)
14080 IF GTMP <> NIL THEN 14060
14090 ' out of space: try pruning
14100 IF LEAFHD = NIL THEN 14200
14110 GTMP=LEAFHD
14120 IF S(S(GTMP+LEAFLST)+LEAFLST) = NIL THEN 14150
14130 GTMP=S(GTMP+LEAFLST)
14140 GOTO 14120
14150 ' leaf with smallest H(x) found: trash it
14160 PLOC=S(GTMP+LEAFLST)
14170 GOSUB 13000:' gosub PUTBACK
14180 S(GTMP+LEAFLST)=NIL
14190 GOTO 14050
14200 ' no memory left: abort program
14210 PRINT:PRINT "OUT OF MEMORY!"
14220 STOP
14230 ' successful search
```

```
14240 GLOC=GTMP+S(GTMP+SIZE)-NEED
14250 S(GLOC+SIZE)=NEED
14260 S(GTMP+SIZE)=S(GTMP+SIZE)-NEED
14270 RETURN
15000 '
15001 '
15002 ' Debugging message:
15003 '
15010 PRINT "push*";
15011 '
15020 ' subroutine PUSH
15030 ' push node KID onto stack
15040 NEED=STKNEED
15050 GOSUB 14000:' gosub GETSTORE
15060 S(GLOC+ORGIDX)=KID
15070 S(GLOC+PTR)=STKHD
15080 STKHD=GLOC
15090 RETURN
16000 '
16001 '
16002 ' Debugging message:
16003 '
16010 PRINT "pop*";
16011 '
16020 ' subroutine POP
16030 ' pop top node off stack
16040 ' (presumed it's already processed)
16050 POPTMP=S(STKHD+PTR)
16060 PLOC=STKHD
16070 GOSUB 13000:' gosub PUTBACK
16080 STKHD=POPTMP
16090 RETURN
17000 '
17001 '
17002 ' Debugging message:
17003 '
17010 PRINT "inithash*";
17011 '
17020 ' subroutine INITHASH
17030 ' initialize hash table HTABLE
17040 ' each table entry points to nil list
17050 NEED=30
17060 GOSUB 14000:' gosub GETSTORE
17070 HTABLE=GLOC
```

```
17080 NEED=LSTNEED
17090 FOR HIN=1 TO 29
17100    S(HTABLE+HIN)=NIL
17110    NEXT HIN
17120 RETURN
18000 ´
18001 ´
18002 ´ Debugging message:
18003 ´
18010 PRINT "heuristic*";
18011 ´
18020 ´ subroutine HEURISTIC
18030 ´ computer heuristic value of HNODE = HX
18040 ´ P1 = # correct position  : A1 = 1
18050 ´ P2 = total Manhattan Dx  : A2 =-1
18060 ´ P3 = sequency            : A3 = 1
18070 ´ P4 = modular correctness : A4 = 1
18080 ´                          : AL =-1
18090 ´ HX = A1*P1 + ... + A4*P4 + AL*S(HNODE+LEVEL)
18100 DP=HNODE+STATE
18110 P1=0:P2=0:P3=0:P4=0
18120 FOR HH = 1 TO 9
18130 ´ P1
18140    IF S(DP+HH) = GOAL(HH) THEN P1=P1+1
18150 ´ P2
18160    HLOC=1
18170    IF GOAL(HLOC) <> S(DP+HH) THEN HLOC=HLOC+1:GOTO 18170
18180    P2=P2+ABS(FNX (HH)-FNX (HLOC))+ABS(FNY (HH)-FNY (HLOC))
18190 ´ P3
18200    IF S(DP+HH+SEQ(HH)) = ((S(DP+HH)+1)MOD 9) THEN P3=P3+1
18210 ´ P4
18220    IF (S(DP+HH) MOD 2) = (GOAL(HH) MOD 2) THEN P4=P4+1
18230    NEXT HH
18240 HX=A1*P1 + A2*P2 + A3*P3 + A4*P4 + AL*S(HNODE+LEVEL)
18250 RETURN
19000 ´
19001 ´
19002 ´ Debugging message:
19003 ´
19010 PRINT "eqstate*";
19011 ´
19020 ´ subroutine EQSTATE
19030 ´ EQSTATE := QREC1.state = QREC2.state
19040 EQSTATE=FALSE
```

```
19050 QI=1
19060 IF S(QREC1+STATE+QI) <> S(QREC2+STATE+QI) THEN RETURN
19070 QI=QI+1
19080 IF QI <= 9 THEN 19060
19090 EQSTATE=TRUE
19100 RETURN
20000 '
20001 '
20002 ' Debugging message:
20003 '
20010 PRINT "hash*";
20011 '
20020 ' subroutine HASH
20030 ' generate hash value HTOT for HNODE
20040 HTOT=0
20050 FOR HI=1 TO 9
20060    HTOT=HTOT+(S(HNODE+STATE+HI)*HI)
20070    NEXT HI
20080 HTOT=INT(((RGM*HTOT)-INT(RGM*HTOT))*29+1)
20090 ' see Knuth,"Art of Computer Pgming, V3" pg 512
20100 RETURN
21000 '
21001 '
21002 ' Debugging message:
21003 '
21010 PRINT "add to closed*";
21011 '
21020 ' subroutine ADCLOSED
21030 ' add node CNODE to closed list
21040 ' list is indexed through hash table HTABLE
21050 ' resolve collisions with fifo stack
21060 NEED = LSTNEED
21070 GOSUB 14000:' gosub GETSTORE
21080 HNODE = GLOC
21090 HTMP=S(HTABLE+ S(CNODE+HASH))
21100 S(HNODE+ORGIDX)=CNODE
21110 ' push onto list
21120 IF HTMP <> NIL THEN 21170
21130 ' nil list
21140 S(HTABLE+ S(CNODE+HASH))=HNODE
21150 S(HNODE+PTR)=NIL
21160 RETURN
21170 ' non-nil list
21180 QREC1=HASHDX
```

```
21190 QREC2=S(HTMP+ORGIDX)
21200 GOSUB 19000:' gosub EQSTATE
21210 IF EQSTATE THEN 21300:' check for clone and return
21220 IF S(HTMP+PTR) <> NIL THEN 21270
21230 ' end of list
21240 S(HTMP+PTR)=HNODE
21250 S(HNODE+PTR)=NIL
21260 RETURN
21270 ' look at next node
21280 HTMP=S(HTMP+PTR)
21290 GOTO 21190
21300 ' check for duplicate node
21310 GOSUB 25000:' gosub LOOPNODES
21320 STOP
21330 RETURN
22000 '
22001 '
22002 ' Debugging message:
22003 '
22010 PRINT "findnode*";
22011 '
22020 ' subroutine FINDNODE
22030 ' find another node with state given in QREC2
22040 ' node found is NODEFND (=NIL if not found)
22050 HNODE=QREC2
22060 NODEFND=NIL
22070 IF S(HTABLE+S(QREC2+HASH)) = NIL THEN RETURN
22080 FT=S(HTABLE+HTOT)
22090 QREC1=S(FT+ORGIDX)
22100 GOSUB 19000:' gosub EQSTATE
22110 IF EQSTATE THEN NODEFND=QREC1:RETURN
22120 IF S(FT+PTR) = NIL THEN RETURN
22130 FT=S(FT+PTR)
22140 GOTO 22090
23000 '
23001 '
23002 ' Debugging message:
23003 '
23010 PRINT "makekid*";
23011 '
23020 ' subroutine MAKEKID
23030 ' make child KID from parent DAD using MVNUM
23040 ' KID=NIL if move not possible
23050 ' first find the blank:
```

```
23060 MK=1
23070 IF S(DAD+STATE+MK) = 0 THEN 23100
23080 MK=MK+1:GOTO 23070
23090 KID=NIL
23100 ' check for illegal moves first
23110 IF (MVNUM=1) AND (MK<4) THEN RETURN
23120 IF (MVNUM=2) AND ((MK MOD 3)=0) THEN RETURN
23130 IF (MVNUM=3) AND (MK>6) THEN RETURN
23140 IF (MVNUM=4) AND ((MK MOD 3)=1) THEN RETURN
23150 ' else move is legal
23160 NEED=NODENEED
23170 GOSUB 14000:' gosub GETSTORE
23180 KID=GLOC
23190 FOR MI=1 TO 9
23200    S(KID+STATE+MI)=S(DAD+STATE+MI)
23210    NEXT MI
23220 ON MVNUM GOTO 23230,23240,23250,23260
23230 MV=-3:GOTO 23270
23240 MV= 1:GOTO 23270
23250 MV= 3:GOTO 23270
23260 MV=-1:GOTO 23270
23270 SWAP S(KID+STATE+MK), S(KID+STATE+MK+MV)
23280 S(KID+LEVEL)=S(DAD+LEVEL)+1
23290 S(KID+FATHER)=DAD
23300 S(KID+OPRTN)=MVNUM
23310 HNODE=KID
23320 GOSUB 18000:' gosub HEURISTIC
23330 S(KID+HEUR)=HX
23340 GOSUB 20000:' gosub HASH
23350 S(KID+HASH)=HTOT
23360 S(KID+EXPLRD)=FALSE
23370 RETURN
24000 '
24001 '
24002 ' Debugging message:
24003 '
24010 PRINT "addkids*";
24011 '
24020 ' subroutine ADDKIDS
24030 ' push kids of DAD onto stack; called from LOOPNODES
24040 FOR MVNUM=1 TO 4
24050    GOSUB 23000:' gosub MAKEKIDS
24060    IF KID = NIL THEN 24140
24070    QREC2=KID
```

```
24080     GOSUB 22000:' gosub FINDNODE
24090     IF NODEFND = NIL THEN 24140
24100     PLOC=KID
24110     GOSUB 13000:' gosub PUTBACK
24120     KID=NODEFND
24130     GOSUB 15000:' gosub PUSH
24140     NEXT MVNUM
24150 RETURN
25000 '
25001 '
25002 ' Debugging message:
25003 '
25010 PRINT "loopnodes*";
25011 '
25020 ' subroutine LOOPNODES
25030 ' if node LNODE exists already, loop tree
25040 QREC2=LNODE
25050 GOSUB 22000:' gosub FINDNODE
25060 IF NODEFND = NIL THEN RETURN
25070 IF S(LNODE+LEVEL) >= S(NODEFND+LEVEL) THEN RETURN
25080 ' better level found: loop
25090 S(NODEFND+FATHER)=S(LNODE+FATHER)
25100 S(NODEFND+LEVEL)=S(LNODE+LEVEL)
25110 IF S(NODEFND+EXPLRD)=FALSE THEN RETURN
25120 ' node was explored: update children
25130 ' initialize
25140 NEED=STKNEED
25150 GOSUB 14000:' gosub GETSTORE
25160 STKHD=GLOC
25170 S(STKHD+PTR)=NIL
25180 S(STKHD+ORGIDX)=NIL
25190 ' update
25200 DAD=NODEFND
25210 GOSUB 24000:' gosub ADDKIDS
25220 KID=S(STKHD+ORGIDX)
25230 IF KID=NIL THEN RETURN
25240 S(KID+LEVEL)=S(S(KID+FATHER)+LEVEL)+1
25250 IF S(KID+EXPLRD) = FALSE THEN 25280
25260 DAD=KID
25270 GOSUB 24000:' gosub ADDKIDS
25280 GOSUB 16000:' gosub POP
25290 GOTO 25220
26000 '
26001 '
```

```
26002 ' Debugging message:
26003 '
26010 PRINT "link2list*";
26011 '
26020 ' subroutine LINK_TO_LIST
26030 ' inserts LNODE into list headed by LEAFHD
26040 ' list sorted in descending heuristic order
26050 IF S(LEAFHD+PTR)<>NIL THEN 26100
26060 ' empty list
26070 S(LEAFHD+PTR)=LNODE
26080 S(LNODE+PTR)=NIL
26090 RETURN
26100 ' non-empty list
26110 L2L1=LEAFHD
26120 L2L2=S(LEAFHD+PTR)
26130 IF S(LNODE+HEUR) > S(L2L2+HEUR) THEN 26230
26140 IF S(L2L2+PTR)=NIL THEN 26190
26150 ' look further down the list
26160 L2L1=L2L2
26170 L2L2=S(L2L2+PTR)
26180 GOTO 26130
26190 ' end of list
26200 S(L2L2+PTR)=LNODE
26210 S(LNODE+PTR)=NIL
26220 RETURN
26230 ' spot found in middle of list
26240 S(L2L1+PTR)=LNODE
26250 S(LNODE+PTR)=L2L2
26260 RETURN
27000 '
27010 ' subroutine PRINTNODE
27020 ' prints node PNODE
27030 PRINT
27040 PRINT " PTR:";S(PNODE+PTR)," LVL:";S(PNODE+LEVEL)," DAD:";S
      (PNODE+FATHER),
27050 PRINT "ADDR:";KID
27060 PRINT "OPTN:";S(PNODE+OPRTN),"HEUR:";S(PNODE+HEUR),"HASH:";S
      (PNODE+HASH),
27070 PRINT "XPLD:";:IF S(PNODE+EXPLRD)=TRUE THEN PRINT " TRUE":GOTO
      27090
27080 PRINT " FALSE"
27090 FOR PI=1 TO 9
27100    PRINT S(PNODE+STATE+PI);"  ";
27110    IF (PI MOD 3) = 0 THEN PRINT
```

```
27120   NEXT PI
27130 RETURN
28000 '
28010 ' subroutine PRINT OPEN NODES
28020 TOP=LEAFHD
28030 PRINT:PRINT "Open nodes (in sorted order):"
28040 IF S(TOP+PTR)=NIL THEN RETURN
28050 PRINT S(TOP+PTR),
28060 TOP=S(TOP+PTR)
28070 GOTO 28040
29000 '
29010 ' miscellaneous subroutines
29020 '
29030 ' printer => console
29040 POKE 3,128:RETURN
29050 ' console => printer
29060 POKE 3,130:RETURN
```

Tiles Data: STARTST.DAT

```
2
8
3
1
6
4
7
0
5
```

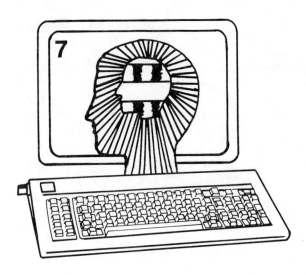

Pattern Recognition

The ability to distinguish desired patterns from a set of data is one of the most important areas of AI development. Its applications extend to a variety of areas, including computer vision, aural input (speech and sound), theorem proving, and planning. It also embodies the classic AI dilemma: how to process large amounts of data when there is very little information about where or in what form the significant data may reside.

In this chapter, we will examine two of the most easily understood algorithms for pattern recognition. One system, the Perceptron, is used to recognize patterns that have been represented as bit-mapped images in a matrix, not unlike the technology used in computer vision. A programming exercise for the ambitious will be given at the end of the chapter. In addition, we will investigate a system for recognizing cursive writing as it is being written, the Ladeen Character Recognizer. This system is unique in that it is more interested in the *sequence* with which patterns are entered, rather than any great amount of *detail* regarding them.

First, however, we will examine one of the strategies by which visual data is represented, and how it may be *smoothed*, or preprocessed, for easier manipulation. It is important to bear in mind that much of the work done in pattern recognition is really a matter of applied statistics, and as such fulfills the cynic's assertion about artificial intelligence: "If it can be done, it was never AI to begin with!"

First the question of how to represent visual data must be made explicit. The specific hardware technology is not particularly relevant, as the final result tends to be the same: some scanning device is trained on the outside world, returning a stream of data in what may initially be either analog or digital form. If it is analog, it must be converted to digital for ease of storage and manipulation. Then the process of smoothing, or preprocessing, begins in earnest.

Naturally, the data received will contain some amount of *noise*, or inaccurate data. The purpose of data smoothing is to eliminate as much of the noisy data as possible, while retaining as much of the good data as possible. Since there is nothing in any one datum that makes it inherently good or bad, algorithms must be devised to allow this process to be automated with a minimum of damage to the good data.

The data will appear in the form of intensity values; they will be placed in a matrix that corresponds to the *field of view* of the scanning device. Each box in this matrix is known as a *pixel*, or *picture element*. The density of the pixels (which may be measured in pixels per square inch) is a measure of the *resolution* of the image; a higher resolution produces a better picture

1.0	1.0	1.0	1.0	1.0	1.0	1.0	1.0	1.0	1.0	1.0	1.0
1.0	1.0	1.0	1.0	1.0	1.0	1.0	1.0	1.0	1.0	1.0	1.0
1.0	1.0	1.0	1.0	1.0	1.0	1.0	1.0	1.0	1.0	1.0	1.0
1.0	1.0	1.0	1.0	1.0	1.0	1.0	1.0	1.0	1.0	1.0	1.0
1.0	1.0	1.0	8.0	8.0	8.0	8.0	8.0	8.0	1.0	1.0	1.0
1.0	1.0	1.0	8.0	8.0	8.0	8.0	8.0	8.0	1.0	1.0	1.0
1.0	1.0	1.0	8.0	8.0	8.0	8.0	8.0	8.0	1.0	1.0	1.0
1.0	1.0	1.0	8.0	8.0	8.0	8.0	8.0	8.0	1.0	1.0	1.0
1.0	1.0	1.0	8.0	8.0	8.0	8.0	8.0	8.0	1.0	1.0	1.0
1.0	1.0	1.0	8.0	8.0	8.0	8.0	8.0	8.0	1.0	1.0	1.0
1.0	1.0	1.0	1.0	1.0	1.0	1.0	1.0	1.0	1.0	1.0	1.0
1.0	1.0	1.0	1.0	1.0	1.0	1.0	1.0	1.0	1.0	1.0	1.0

Fig. 7-1. A pattern without noise.

1.0	1.0	1.0	1.0	1.0	1.0	0.3	1.0	1.0	1.0	1.0	1.0
1.0	1.0	1.0	1.0	1.0	1.0	1.0	1.0	1.0	1.0	1.0	1.0
1.0	1.0	1.0	1.0	1.0	1.0	1.0	1.0	1.4	1.0	1.0	1.0
1.0	0.2	1.0	1.9	1.0	1.0	1.0	1.0	1.0	1.0	1.0	1.0
1.0	1.0	1.0	8.0	8.0	8.0	8.0	8.0	7.8	1.0	1.0	1.0
1.0	1.0	0.7	8.2	8.0	8.0	8.0	8.0	7.8	1.0	1.0	1.0
1.0	1.0	0.9	7.7	8.0	8.0	8.0	8.0	8.0	1.0	1.0	1.0
1.0	1.0	1.0	7.9	8.0	8.0	8.0	8.0	8.0	1.0	1.0	1.0
1.0	1.0	1.0	8.0	8.0	7.4	8.0	8.0	8.0	1.0	1.0	1.0
1.0	1.0	1.0	8.0	8.0	8.0	7.6	8.0	8.0	0.4	1.0	1.0
1.0	1.0	1.0	1.0	1.0	1.0	1.0	1.0	1.0	1.1	1.0	1.0
1.0	1.0	1.0	1.0	1.0	1.0	1.0	1.0	1.0	1.0	1.0	1.0

Fig. 7-2. A mildly noisy pattern.

in theory, but it requires greater storage and processing capacity.

Let us presume that the brighter a pixel, the higher its value will be. If we were examining an evenly lit picture of a white square on a black background without any noise, the data might be represented as shown in Fig. 7-1.

The square begins in the fifth row and the fourth column, and extends down to the tenth row and ninth column: the values are 8.0. If the image area were 2″ by 2″, the density would be 144 pixels/4 square inches, or 36 pixels/sq in—a very low resolution. In contrast, a high resolution video monitor has about 13,000 pixels/sq in. You can see that the volumes of data can become enormous quite quickly.

It is impossible, however, to get "pure" data in, unless you have coded it by hand—which was in fact a common practice in the early days of AI research. A mildly noisy version of the above pattern is shown in Fig. 7-2. Notice in this case that while most of the numbers are still either 1.0 or 8.0, about 10 percent have been replaced with values that are slightly off the norms. This represents a relatively clear picture, nonetheless; a truly noisy picture would have a greater number of disturbed pixels, and the degree of variance would be much greater.

Remember as well that the computer has no way of knowing which pixels are noisier than the others, or what the "real" pattern is supposed to be. So, we must help it along in the best way that we can, trying to preserve the original data as we eliminate the noise.

The simplest, and usually best, way of filtering out the noise is to take a number of readings of the same subject and average them together. This is fine if the subject is not moving too quickly (such that there is a shift in the matrix of the various values), and of course there must be the input and processing time available to retrieve and manipulate the thousands of pixels that will be in question.

A less satisfactory method, but often the only one available, is that of *smoothing*. Smoothing involves deciding upon a *neighborhood* for each pixel and then using some method of taking into account the values of a pixel's neighbors in helping to determine the final value for each pixel. One method is to weight the value of each of neighbors in proportion to their closeness of the pixel in question. For example, let us assume that the neighbors under consideration are the eight pixels that are adjacent to the pixel in question horizontally, vertically, and diagonally. This would yield the "map" of the neighborhood shown in Fig. 7-3.

In this case, each neighbor is labeled with the distance between it and the pixel in question, which is arbitrarily labeled (.5). In order to compute the smoothed value for the pixel, each of the neighbor's values is divided by its distance, then added to a total. The pixel's own value is doubled (divided by 0.5), and included in the sum. The result is then stored in the new, smoothed matrix, and the next pixel is processed, until every pixel has been smoothed. Figure 7-4 shows the result that would be obtained by using this method on the matrix in Fig. 7-2.

You may notice that the values stored in the smoothed matrix are approximately 9 times larger than in the original, "raw" matrix. Normally,

Fig. 7-3. A pixel under consideration and its eight neighbors.

1.41	1.00	1.41
1.00	(.5)	1.00
1.41	1.00	1.41

this is not considered to be a problem, since the broad relationships remain constant. The reason for not doing the final division by 8.837 to bring them back to "normal" is that this is yet another operation that must be performed on each pixel, and an expensive one computationally speaking. Thus, the altered values are usually left to remain "as is" in the new matrix.

What is more significant, however, is that the "crispness" of the original box, even in the noisy example, has been lost. It has, literally, been smoothed out; such is the price one pays for a rather poor smoothing algorithm. Another problem that has arisen is that "artifacts" have appeared on the edges, giving the appearance of objects when none are there. Further preprocessing will be necessary to remove these artifacts.

Now, we are ready for the business of finding the square. Ideally, what is a square? It is a four-sided shape, where each of the sides is equal, and at right angles to each other. When searching for a square, we are not so much interested in the center; we want to know the details of the edges. Since this approach will be useful in a variety of applications, a number of algorithms have arisen for finding the edges in a picture, the most common of which is the *LaPlace transform*.

4.7	6.4	6.4	6.4	6.4	6.4	6.4	6.4	6.4	6.4	6.4	4.7
6.4	8.8	8.8	8.8	8.8	8.8	8.8	8.8	8.8	8.8	8.8	6.4
6.4	8.8	8.8	8.8	8.8	8.8	8.8	8.8	8.8	8.8	8.8	6.4
6.4	8.8	13.8	20.8	25.7	25.7	25.7	25.7	20.8	13.8	8.8	6.4
6.4	8.8	20.8	41.8	53.7	53.7	53.7	53.7	41.8	20.8	8.8	6.4
6.4	8.8	25.7	53.7	70.6	70.6	70.6	70.6	53.7	25.7	8.8	6.4
6.4	8.8	25.7	53.7	70.6	70.6	70.6	70.6	53.7	25.7	8.8	6.4
6.4	8.8	25.7	53.7	70.6	70.6	70.6	70.6	53.7	25.7	8.8	6.4
6.4	8.8	25.7	53.7	70.6	70.6	70.6	70.6	53.7	25.7	8.8	6.4
6.4	8.8	20.8	41.8	53.7	53.7	53.7	53.7	41.8	20.8	8.8	6.4
6.4	8.8	13.8	20.8	25.7	25.7	25.7	25.7	20.8	13.8	8.8	6.4
4.7	6.4	6.4	6.4	6.4	6.4	6.4	6.4	6.4	6.4	6.4	4.7

Fig. 7-4. A smoothed matrix.

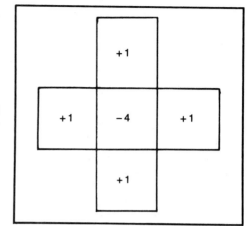

Fig. 7-5. The significant neighbors
when the LaPlace transform is used.

The strategy of the LaPlace transform is to highlight those areas of the picture where changes between light and dark take place: these will be the edges, and once they are known, further analysis of them can be made.

In the LaPlace algorithm, the neighborhood is somewhat more restricted than in the smoothing example we used above. Here, a pixel has only four neighbors: up, down, right, and left. Their values are summed, as in the smoothing algorithm, after being multiplied by the factors shown in Fig. 7-5.

The result here is that if a pixel has four neighbors identical to itself, its final value will be zero. However, if two of the neighboring pixels (for example) are significantly different, then the final value will be correspondingly greater (or less) than zero.

When plotting the results, only the absolute value of the pixels is considered, as it is the magnitude of difference that is being looked for, not the specific values. A threshold must also be taken into consideration, for matters of contrast. A lower threshold of difference to be plotted will result in less contrast, and more apparent edges; a higher threshold will have the reverse effect. Taking the two matrices above (one smoothed, the other not), let us see what happens when the LaPlace transform is applied to them. First, Fig. 7-6 shows the smoothed matrix and its graphic representation.

The representations of the matrix are simply constructed by assigning an underscore to those values that fall below the threshold and a star to those that are greater. Notice the artifacts at the lower thresholds and the lack of lines at the greater. For this smoothing algorithm, the optimal threshold would appear to be about 18. Now let us examine the matrix that was not smoothed, as shown in Fig. 7-7.

In this case, the optimal threshold is somewhere around 6.0, as the sides are still in evidence, despite their apparent thickness.

THE PERCEPTRON

Now that we have the strategy by which we will store the visual data

121

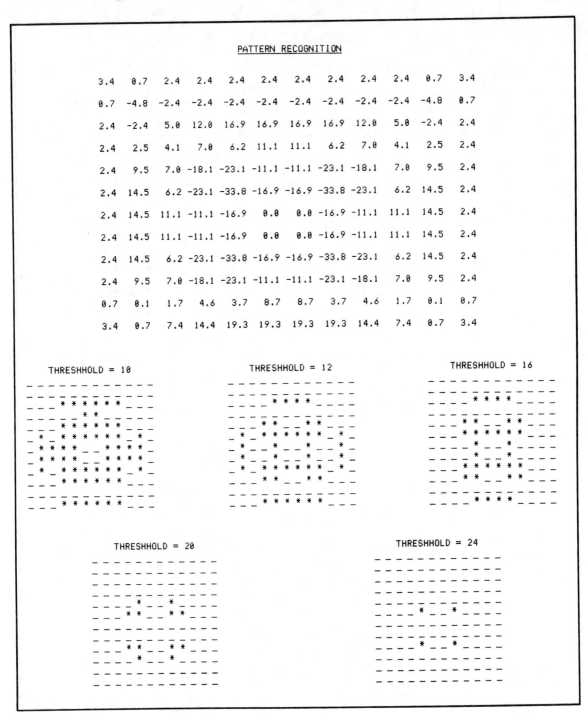

Fig. 7-6. The form diminishes as the threshold increases.

PATTERN RECOGNITION

```
 0.0   0.0   0.0   0.0   0.0  -0.7   2.1  -0.7   0.0   0.0   0.0   0.0

 0.0   0.0   0.0   0.0   0.0   0.0  -0.7   0.0   0.4   0.0   0.0   0.0

 0.0  -0.8   0.0   0.9   0.0   0.0   0.0   0.4  -1.6   0.4   0.0   0.0

-0.8   3.1   0.1   3.5   7.9   7.0   7.0   7.0   7.2   0.0   0.0   0.0

 0.0  -0.8   6.7 -12.9  -7.0  -7.0  -7.0  -7.2 -13.5   6.8   0.0   0.0

 0.0  -0.3   8.3  -8.4   0.2   0.0   0.0  -0.2  -6.3   6.8   0.0   0.0

 0.0  -0.1   6.8  -5.8  -0.3   0.0   0.0   0.0  -7.2   7.0   0.0   0.0

 0.0   0.0   6.8  -7.0  -0.1  -0.6   0.0   0.0  -7.0   7.0   0.0   0.0

 0.0   0.0   7.0  -7.1  -0.6   2.3  -1.0   0.0  -7.0   6.4   0.0   0.0

 0.0   0.0   7.0 -14.0  -7.0  -8.0  -5.5  -7.4 -14.6   9.4  -0.6   0.0

 0.0   0.0   0.0   7.0   7.0   7.0   6.6   7.0   7.1  -1.0   0.1   0.0

 0.0   0.0   0.0   0.0   0.0   0.0   0.0   0.0   0.0   0.1   0.0   0.0
```

```
THRESHHOLD = 5              THRESHHOLD = 6              THRESHHOLD = 7
- - - - - - - - - - - -     - - - - - - - - - - - -     - - - - - - - - - - - -
- - - - - - - - - - - -     - - - - - - - - - - - -     - - - - - - - - - - - -
- - * * * * * - - -         - - - * * * * * - - -       - - - - * - - - * - - -
- * * * * * * * - -         - - * * * * * * * - -       - - - * - * - * * - -
- * * - - - * * - -         - - * * - - - * * - -       - - * * - - - - - - -
- * * - - - * * - -         - * - - - - - * * - -       - - - - - - - * - - -
- * * - - - * * - -         - * - - - - - * * - -       - - - - - - - - - - -
- * * - - - * * - -         - * * - - - - * * - -       - - - * - - - - - - -
- * * * * * * * - -         - - * * * * - * * * - -     - - - * - * - * * * - -
- - * * * * * * - - -       - - - * * * * * * - - -     - - - - - - - * - - -
- - - - - - - - - - - -     - - - - - - - - - - - -     - - - - - - - - - - - -
```

```
        THRESHHOLD = 7.25                   THRESHHOLD = 7.5
- - - - - - - - - - - -             - - - - - - - - - - - -
- - - - - - - - - - - -             - - - - - - - - - - - -
- - - * - - - - - - -               - - - * - - - - - - -
- - - * - - - - * - - -             - - - * - - - * - - -
- - * * - - - - - - -               - - * * - - - - - - -
- - - - - - - - - - - -             - - - - - - - - - - - -
- - - - - - - - - - - -             - - - - - - - - - - - -
- - - * - * - * * * - -             - - - * - * - * * - -
- - - - - - - - - - - -             - - - - - - - - - - - -
- - - - - - - - - - - -             - - - - - - - - - - - -
```

Fig. 7-7. Again, the form diminishes as the threshold increases.

and a brief understanding of the processes necessary to make use of it, let us proceed to the problem of recognizing patterns within the data training the program from scratch, so that it can recognize any set of patterns that we wish.

In doing so, we will be using a classic pattern recognition program known as the *Perceptron*, which was first proposed by Rosenblatt in 1957 [1]. The Perceptron falls into that unfortunate category of successful AI applications that was quickly branded as not being "real" AI, simply because it worked and the algorithm was simple to understand. It nonetheless presents an interesting glimpse into the ways that programs can be made to perform as if they are learning, without worrying about whether they are actually learning or not.

In the case of Perceptron, the idea is to take a number of digitized letters and program the computer to recognize them, even with a certain amount of noise in the data. Furthermore, the program will be "trained" to recognize these noisy patterns, and will thus be able to become as accurate a pattern recognizer as the amount of time the human can spend on training will allow.

As mentioned previously, the data for these sessions was initially coded by hand. This was more practical than spending time arranging for and debugging a hardware system to generate the data. Furthermore, data was represented, not as a range of pixel values, but as either 0s or 1s, with 1s representing dark pixels and 0s light pixels. A series of letters, such as the letter shown in Fig. 7-8 was hand-coded.

The pattern was labeled as the pure A, for later reference. It was then reproduced into several noisy copies, or matrices in which some of the 0s were changed to 1s, and vice versa. It was these noisy versions that were used to train the Perceptron.

Each letter of the alphabet was similarly encoded, made noisy, and labeled with the letter of the alphabet that it represented. These completed records—a matrix and a label each—were then placed into a training set. When the alphabet was complete, the training mode was entered, and the Perceptron began to "learn the alphabet".

Let us presume that there were 100 noisy copies of each letter, or 2600 patterns altogether. In the program, a set of 26 matrices—one for each letter—was set aside, each containing all 0s; an additional field was set aside for the label that indicated which letter that pattern represented. Each pattern from the training set would be read in, and then the value of each pixel in the noisy pattern would be multiplied by the corresponding pixel in each of the Perceptron's 26 matrices. After each matrix had been processed against the noisy pattern in this manner, the values generated were totaled for each matrix, and the highest value was the guess made by the Perceptron as the intended letter. If guess was correct, no further processing was performed, and the next training pattern was read in.

```
0  0  0  0  0  0  0  0  0  0  0

0  0  0  0  0  0  0  0  0  0  0

0  0  0  0  0  1  0  0  0  0  0

0  0  0  0  1  0  1  0  0  0  0

0  0  0  1  0  0  0  1  0  0  0

0  0  0  1  1  1  1  1  0  0  0

0  0  1  0  0  0  0  0  1  0  0

0  0  1  0  0  0  0  0  1  0  0

0  0  1  0  0  0  0  0  1  0  0

0  0  0  0  0  0  0  0  0  0  0

0  0  0  0  0  0  0  0  0  0  0
```

Fig. 7-8. The pattern representing the letter A.

If, however, the Perceptron guessed incorrectly, the values in the training matrix would be added to the intended matrix in the Perceptron, and a flag would be set to indicate that there had been a failure in that training run. Then the remaining test matrices would be processed, until all of the 2600 matrices had been tested. If there had been a failure in the training run, the entire training run was repeated, over and over, until a flawless run was achieved.

The validation stage was then begun: a second set of noisy patterns was generated from the original masters, in the same manner as before. Then the Perceptron was tested with this new set, which could be as large or noisy as desired to maximize the accuracy of the final results. If the Perceptron processed this validation set flawlessly, it was deemed to have "learned" the patterns to the degree intended. Otherwise, this new validation set was used as a training set, and the entire process was repeated.

The principle utilized in the Perceptron is that the patterns had to be what is known as *linearly separable*, or distinguishable by a simple mathematic function. The notion corresponds to that of a map on which there are certain clusters of objects that you want to separate by drawing straight lines, as shown in Fig. 7-9.

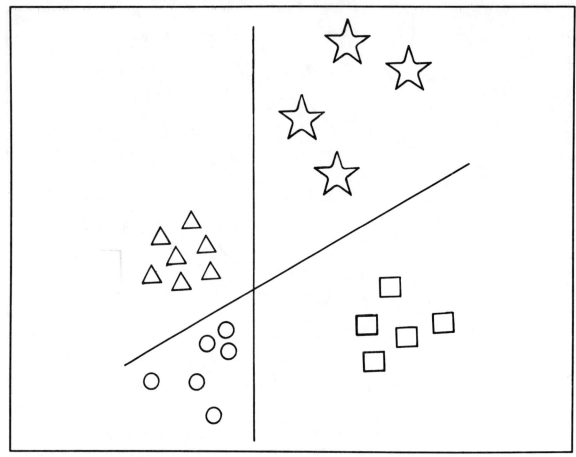

Fig. 7-9. A simple cluster diagram.

You will note that the four regions can easily be divided through the use of straight lines, as shown. In Fig. 7-10, however, such a feat is not possible. In this case, curved lines need to be drawn to clearly delineate the clusters of similar objects. In the above example, there are two dimensions—height and width—and so it is not difficult to arrive at patterns of clusters that will require curved lines to separate them. In the perceptron, however, each pixel represents another (mathematical) dimension by which the figure can be expressed. So, for the pattern set used earlier—11×11—we would be representing each cluster in 121 dimensions, making it quite difficult to arrive at clusters which could not be separated by a series of straight lines.

Now, the number of pixels, or the resolution of the image, will correspond directly to the accuracy that can be achieved by the Perceptron, in conjunction with the amount of noise that is allowed into the patterns and

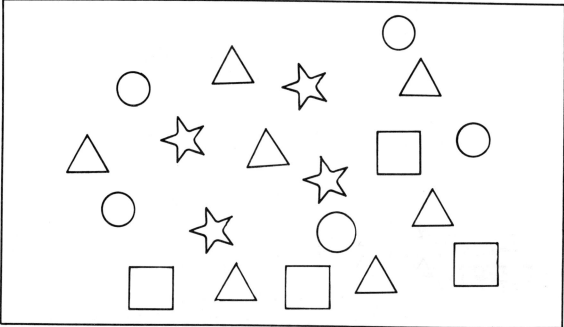

Fig. 7-10. A more complex cluster diagram.

the number of test patterns used. The greater the accuracy desired, the greater the computational requirements. While this was a serious consideration in the 50s and 60s, this is no longer the case, and the Perceptron is a viable manner of pattern recognition for today's computers.

A programming example is given at the end of this chapter for the interested reader; however, a single pass of the testing phase of the Perceptron may prove useful in conceptualizing the process involved. For our example we will use a very small sample set, two patterns represented in a 4 × 4 matrix, and a very small test set, three patterns each. The two pat-

Fig. 7-11. Two pure patterns.

```
           PATTERN RECOGNITION
    1  1  1  1        1  0  0  0

    1  0  0  1        0  1  0  0

    1  0  0  1        0  0  1  0

    1  1  1  1        0  0  0  1

       SQUARE            DIAGONAL
```

terns are shown in Fig. 7-11. They can also be represented in an array by taking each of the rows in turn, as:

SQUARE:

1 1 1 1 1 0 0 1 1 0 0 1 1 1 1 1

DIAGONAL:

1 0 0 0 0 1 0 0 0 0 1 0 0 0 0 1

This is done for ease of computation.

We will first create three noisy patterns for each of the two patterns:

S1:
1 1 1 1 1 1 0 1 1 0 0 1 1 1 1 0

S2:
1 1 1 1 1 0 0 1 1 0 0 0 1 1 0 1

S3:
1 1 1 0 1 0 0 1 1 0 0 1 1 1 0 1

D1:
1 0 1 0 0 1 0 0 0 0 1 0 1 0 0 1

D2:
0 0 0 0 0 1 0 0 0 0 1 0 0 0 1 1

D3:
1 0 0 0 0 1 0 0 0 0 1 0 1 0 1 1

These patterns in our binary representation are shown in Fig. 7-12. You will notice that each of the patterns has had two of its pixels "flipped" to represent the noise in the pattern.

To begin the training process, we must select an order for the patterns to be presented to the Perceptron for training. To maintain diversity, we shall alternate between Squares and Diagonals; thus, the order will be:

S1; D1; S2; D2; S3; D3

We will also initialize two "training" matrices to all zeroes, calling them TS and TD. Taking the first pattern, we process it with each of the two

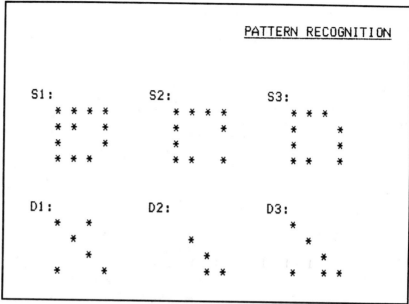

Fig. 7-12. Some noisy versions of the pure patterns.

training matrices as described above: each element of the noisy pattern is multiplied by its corresponding element in the training pattern. As the process continues, a running sum is kept. At the end, after both training matrices have been processed, the larger sum will be the guess made as to which pattern has been "observed." In the case of a tie, the square will be chosen (arbitrarily).

The first pass looks like this:

```
TS:   0   0   0   0   0   0   0   0   0   0   0   0   0   0   0   0
S1:   1   1   1   1   1   1   0   1   1   0   0   1   1   1   1   0
      ─────────────────────────────────────────────────────────────
      0   0   0   0   0   0   0   0   0   0   0   0   0   0   0   0
sumS=0


TD:   0   0   0   0   0   0   0   0   0   0   0   0   0   0   0   0
S1:   1   1   1   1   1   1   0   1   1   0   0   1   1   1   1   0
      ─────────────────────────────────────────────────────────────
      0   0   0   0   0   0   0   0   0   0   0   0   0   0   0   0
sumD=0
```

Since both sums are zero, Square is chosen, which is correct. No further processing is done, and the second test pattern is chosen (D1):

```
TS:  0  0  0  0  0  0  0  0  0  0  0  0  0  0  0  0
D1:  1  0  1  0  0  1  0  0  0  0  1  0  1  0  0  1
----------------------------------------------------
     0  0  0  0  0  0  0  0  0  0  0  0  0  0  0  0
sumS=0

TD:  0  0  0  0  0  0  0  0  0  0  0  0  0  0  0  0
D1:  1  0  1  0  0  1  0  0  0  0  1  0  1  0  0  1
----------------------------------------------------
     0  0  0  0  0  0  0  0  0  0  0  0  0  0  0  0
sumD=0
```

Again, both sums are zero, and Square is chosen; however, this is incorrect, so the Perceptron must be "trained" for recognizing Diagonals. This is done by adding the test pattern to TD (since it was supposed to have guessed D):

```
TD:  0  0  0  0  0  0  0  0  0  0  0  0  0  0  0  0
D1:  1  0  1  0  0  1  0  0  0  0  1  0  1  0  0  1
----------------------------------------------------
TD=  1  0  1  0  0  1  0  0  0  0  1  0  1  0  0  1
```

Now the next pattern, S2, is processed:

```
TS:  0  0  0  0  0  0  0  0  0  0  0  0  0  0  0  0
S2:  1  1  1  1  1  0  0  1  1  0  0  0  1  1  0  1
----------------------------------------------------
     0  0  0  0  0  0  0  0  0  0  0  0  0  0  0  0
sumS=0

TD:  1  0  1  0  0  1  0  0  0  0  1  0  1  0  0  1
S2:  1  1  1  1  1  0  0  1  1  0  0  0  1  1  0  1
----------------------------------------------------
     1  0  1  0  0  0  0  0  0  0  0  0  1  0  0  1
sumD=4
```

In this case, sumD is chosen, as it is the larger of the two. But this is incorrect, so training must be done for Squares:

```
TS:  0  0  0  0  0  0  0  0  0  0  0  0  0  0  0  0
S2:  1  1  1  1  1  0  0  1  1  0  0  0  1  1  0  1
----------------------------------------------------
TS=  1  1  1  1  1  0  0  1  1  0  0  0  1  1  0  1
```

The next pattern, D2, is processed:

```
TS:  1  1  1  1  1  0  0  1  1  0  0  0  1  1  0  1
D2:  0  0  0  0  0  1  0  0  0  0  1  0  0  0  1  1
_____
     0  0  0  0  0  0  0  0  0  0  0  0  0  0  0  1
sumS=1
```

```
TD:  1  0  1  0  0  1  0  0  0  0  1  0  1  0  0  1
D2:  0  0  0  0  0  1  0  0  0  0  1  0  0  0  1  1
_____
     0  0  0  0  0  1  0  0  0  0  1  0  0  0  0  1
sumD=3
```

SumD is larger than sumS, and so Diagonal is chosen. This is correct, and no training is done. The next pattern is S3:

```
TS:  1  1  1  1  1  0  0  1  1  0  0  0  1  1  0  1
S3:  1  1  1  0  1  0  0  1  1  0  0  1  1  1  0  1
_____
     1  1  1  0  1  0  0  1  1  0  0  0  1  1  0  1
sumS=9
```

```
TD:  1  0  1  0  0  1  0  0  0  0  1  0  1  0  0  1
S3:  1  1  1  0  1  0  0  1  1  0  0  1  1  1  0  1
_____
     1  0  1  0  0  0  0  0  0  0  0  0  1  0  0  1
sumD=4
```

Again, a correct choice is made, so no training is done. The final pattern is processed:

```
TS:  1  1  1  1  1  0  0  1  1  0  0  0  1  1  0  1
D3:  1  0  0  0  0  1  0  0  0  0  1  0  1  0  1  1
_____
     1  0  0  0  0  0  0  0  0  0  0  0  1  0  0  1
sumS=3
```

```
TD:  1  0  1  0  0  1  0  0  0  0  1  0  1  0  0  1
D3:  1  0  0  0  0  1  0  0  0  0  1  0  1  0  1  1
_____
     1  0  0  0  0  1  0  0  0  0  1  0  1  0  0  1
sumD=5
```

As before, no training is required, since sumD was larger than sumS, and the proper choice was Diagonal.

If the full training program were to be implemented, the entire test pattern would have to be reprocessed, since there had been at least one error in the run. This would continue until each pattern could be tested without making a single bad guess. Then a new set of noisy patterns would be generated and tested. If they were all guessed correctly, the Perceptron would be complete; otherwise, testing (with the new noisy test set) would have to continue.

Now, this was a trivial example, and the numbers never grew larger than 1. However, it is not unusual in a larger system for the number of errors to be quite large, and the values in each pixel to be correspondingly greater. Also, bear in mind that not only were the two patterns quite different, they each had a different number of "1" pixels: the square had 12, and the diagonal 4. So it is not unreasonable to expect a quick result under these circumstances.

THE LADEEN CHARACTER RECOGNIZER

An entirely different approach to character recognition can be found in the Ladeen Character Recognizer (LCR). Instead of recording the specific pixel values of a character, the process of creating each letter is recorded, encoded, and ultimately processed. It is interesting to note that the methodology used here—that of categorizing letters by their construction rather than by a detailed look at their appearance—is the same method used in Chinese approaches to creating an alphabet. Whether this was an early influence in the development of the Ladeen system is not known.

One of the drawbacks to the LCR is that it is not easily suited to "learning" over a set of noisy data, as is the Perceptron. Nonetheless, its implementation is straightforward and can be used to recognize characters as a person writes them.

The strategy used is that of dividing each letter into a series of strokes and tracking the strokes through a series of large cells in order to follow their sequence. With the Perceptron, the greater the resolution (number of pixels), the greater the ultimate accuracy became. With the LCR, this is not always the case. While a specific number of cells is not always the best, the number may be as small as 9, and 16 cells are probably sufficient.

Let us take, for example, the letter J. It might be drawn as shown in Fig. 7-13, with the strokes numbered and arrowed to indicate the process by which the person drew the letter.

As the letter is being written, a routine monitors the interaction of the stylus with the input device, be it tablet, optical scanning device, or whatever. This routine will be sensitive to every time the stylus is removed from the pad, and record the end (and beginning) of strokes around this event. After all strokes have been recorded, the field is divided into a series of

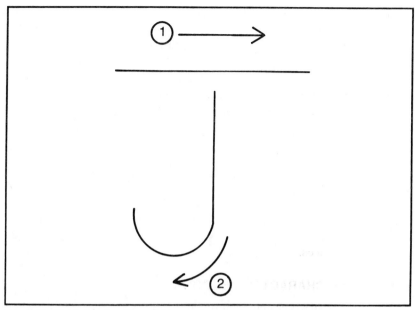

Fig. 7-13. The letter J as it would be analyzed using the Ladeen system.

large cells: in our example, nine. Then each stroke is processed in the following manner.

First, the start cell of the stroke is determined. This is inserted into the first element of a list, or array, for that stroke. Then the stroke is traced in the memory of the computer, each transition from cell to another being recorded in a subsequent element of the list or array.

After all the strokes are recorded, they are linked together under a label for the letter, which contains the number of strokes associated with that letter. Thus, for the letter J, the strokes would be encoded in this way:

        1: 1 2 3
        2: 2 5 8 7 4

And the full code would be something like:

        J: 2
        1: 1 2 3
        2: 2 5 8 7 4
        <eof>

Note that there are several problems with this representation of a character: first of all, there is a critical sensitivity to the positioning of the strokes; that is the reason for using a small number of cells. If a larger number of cells were used, there is the possibility that a small deviation in drawing the letter would result in a different sequence of cells being followed.

A more serious problem is that the LCR is also sensitive to the *order* in which strokes are made. For example, if the hook of the J were drawn first instead of second, then the pattern would look quite different than the first:

```
J: 2
1: 2 5 8 7 4
2: 1 2 3
<eof>
```

Furthermore, the direction is also sensitive: note the difference when the strokes are drawn in the opposite directions:

```
J: 2
1: 3 2 1
2: 4 7 8 5 2
<eof>
```

Now, it is possible for the AI programmer to write routines that test for these type of reversals and out-of-sequence problems, but they both make the code slower and more complex. Thus, the LCR is not in wide use throughout the industry at this time.

What has emerged is a combination of the two approaches: looking at letters first in detail and then examining their structures. Routines similar to those of edge detection in computer vision systems are used to extract the structures, or strokes, from the detailed images. Then these structures are used to construct a description of the letter that more closely corresponds to a verbal (i.e., that is, hopefully human) description of the letter. For example, the letter H can be described as two long vertical bars with a short connecting horizontal bar. Such an approach is described in a recent work by Wong and You [1985], in which they identify six codes for relationships between lines, and describe letters accordingly. The letter H, for example, might be described as:

> Line 1: "Branching with" Line 2
>   "Left of" Line 3
>
> Line 2: "Branching with" Line 3

where "Branching with" is visualized as:

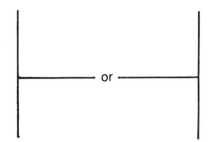

and "Left of" is visualized as:

There are mathematical ways of expressing these relationships that make computerized processing possible but are beyond the scope of this work. The significant result is that approaches like this can be used to take advantage of the way that machinery can access data, the way people think about letters, and the way in which people make letters. And that is truly the goal of artificial intelligence: not to make human machines, but to make machines that capitalize on *both* the strengths of machinery and the strengths of humanity.

For the interested reader, here is the program for the Perceptron, rendered in BASIC. It only uses standard functions in BASIC, so that it should be easily implemented under any reasonably complete version of that language. Also included is the listing of the data file: try your own character sets and see how it functions!

The Perceptron Program

```
1000 '
1010 '
1020 ' SELF-ADAPTIVE PATTERN RECOGNIZER
1030 '
1040 '            Jim Brule'
1050 '            Artificial Intelligence
```

```
1060 '                    Spring, 1984
1070 '
1080 RANDOMIZE
1090 TRUE=(1=1):FALSE=(1=0)
1100 '
1110 ' Open up data file.  Two data sets are to
1120 '    be processed, but flexibility is left
1130 '    for others to be added at a later date.
1140 '
1150 OPEN "I",1,"B:LEARN.DAT"
1160 INPUT#1,NUMSMPLS%
1170 IF NUMSMPLS%=0 THEN 2440
1180 '
1190 ' If not out of data, then continue:
1200 '
1210 INPUT#1,ROW%,COL%,NUMNOYZY%
1220 SMPLSIZE%=ROW%*COL%+1
1230 MAX%=NUMSMPLS%*NUMNOYZY%
1240 '
1250 ' Set up matrices, etc. to hold data internally.
1260 '
1270 DIM SAMPLE(MAX%,SMPLSIZE%):'     holds all noisy samples
1280 DIM LABEL(MAX%):'               holds corresponding labels
1290 DIM D(NUMSMPLS%):'              holds W(i) [dot] S(i)
1300 DIM W(NUMSMPLS%,SMPLSIZE%):'    holds weights
1310 DIM PURE(NUMSMPLS%,SMPLSIZE%):' holds "pure" patterns
1320 '
1330 ' clear weights
1340 '
1350 FOR I=1 TO NUMSMPLS%
1360    FOR J=1 TO SMPLSIZE%
1370      W(1,J)=0
1380      NEXT J
1390    NEXT I
1400 '
1410 ' read pure patterns
1420 '
1430 FOR I=1 TO NUMSMPLS%
1440    FOR J=1 TO SMPLSIZE%
1450      INPUT#1, PURE(I,J)
1460      NEXT J
1470    NEXT I
1480 TRAINING=TRUE
1490 '
```

```
1500 ' print out pure patterns
1510 '
1520 FOR I=1 TO NUMSMPLS%
1530   LPRINT "PATTERN NUMBER";I
1540   FOR R=1 TO ROW%
1550     O$=SPACE$(COL%)
1560     FOR C=1 TO COL%
1570       T=(R-1)*COL% + C
1580       IF PURE(I,T)=1 THEN MID$(O$,C,1)="*"
1590       NEXT C
1600     LPRINT O$
1610     NEXT R
1620   LPRINT
1630   NEXT I
1640 LPRINT:LPRINT:LPRINT
1650 '
1660 ' generate noisy sample
1670 '
1680 CYCLE=0:'                         counts complete tries
1690 L=1
1700 FOR I=1 TO MAX%
1710   FOR J=1 TO SMPLSIZE%:'          first get a pure copy
1720     SAMPLE(I,J)=PURE(L,J)
1730     NEXT J
1740   LABEL(I)=L:'                     establish correct label
1750   R=INT(RND*(SMPLSIZE-1)+1):'      "flip" one location (R)
1760   SAMPLE(I,R)=ABS(SAMPLE(I,R)-1):' clever?
1770   IF RND<.8 THEN 1800:'            "flip" two 20% of the time
1780     R=INT(RND*(SMPLSIZE-1)+1)
1790     SAMPLE(I,R)=ABS(SAMPLE(I,R)-1)
1800   L=L+1:IF L>NUMSMPLS% THEN L=1:'  increment L mod NUMSMPLS%
1810   PRINT "GENERATING SAMPLE";I
1820   NEXT I
1830 '
1840 ' test a complete sample
1850 '
1860 BADGUESS=FALSE
1870 FOR TRY=1 TO MAX%:'                try each sample once
1880   FOR GUESS=1 TO NUMSMPLS%
1890     D(GUESS)=0
1900     FOR I=1 TO SMPLSIZE%
1910       D(GUESS)=D(GUESS) + W(GUESS,I)*SAMPLE(TRY,I)
1920       NEXT I
1930     NEXT GUESS
```

```
1940    BEST=1:'                           look for best guess
1950    FOR I=2 TO NUMSMPLS%
1960      IF D(I) > D(BEST) THEN BEST=I
1970      NEXT I
1980    IF BEST=LABEL(TRY) THEN 2060:'   got it right!
1990      LPRINT "BADGUESS -";BEST;"INSTEAD OF";LABEL(TRY)
2000      BADGUESS=TRUE
2010      IF (NOT TRAINING) THEN TRY=MAX%+1:GOTO 2060:'exit
          loop if not training
2020        FOR I=1 TO SMPLSIZE%:'         retrain here
2030          W(BEST,I)=W(BEST,I)-SAMPLE(TRY,I)
2040          W(LABEL(TRY),I)=W(LABEL(TRY),I)+SAMPLE(TRY,I)
2050          NEXT I
2060      PRINT TRY:NEXT TRY
2070 CYCLE=CYCLE+1
2080 IF TRAINING AND BADGUESS THEN 2120
2090 IF TRAINING AND (NOT BADGUESS) THEN 2170
2100 IF (NOT TRAINING) AND BADGUESS THEN 2250
2110 GOTO 2340:'                          not training; all correct!
2120 '
2130 ' training unsuccessful - try again
2140 '
2150 LPRINT "TRAINING CYCLE";CYCLE;"UNSUCCESSFUL."
2160 GOTO 1860
2170 '
2180 ' training complete - test with new noisy sample
2190 '
2200 TRAINING=FALSE
2210 LPRINT
2220 LPRINT "TRAINING COMPLETE AFTER";CYCLE;"CYCLES."
2230 LPRINT "TESTING IN PROGRESS."
2240 GOTO 1690
2250 '
2260 ' testing fails - retrain using test data
2270 '    (rationale: a new random sample would not guarantee
2280 '                 errors, and therefore it is possible that
2290 '                 no training would take place.)
2300 '
2310 TRAINING=TRUE
2320 LPRINT "TESTING UNSUCCESSFUL - RETRAINING IN PROGRESS."
2330 GOTO 1860
2340 '
2350 ' testing successful - this set done
2360 '
```

```
2370 LPRINT "TESTING SUCCESSFUL!  E.T. PHONE HOME!"
2380 LPRINT:LPRINT
2390 ´
2400 ´ initiate new run
2410 ´
2420 ERASE SAMPLE,LABEL,D,W,PURE
2430 GOTO 1160
2440 CLOSE:END
```

Perceptron Data

```
4,7,5,25
0,0,1,0,0
0,1,1,0,0
0,0,1,0,0
0,0,1,0,0
0,0,1,0,0
0,0,1,0,0
0,1,1,1,0,1
0,1,1,1,0
1,0,0,0,1
0,0,0,0,1
0,0,1,1,0
0,1,1,0,0
1,1,0,0,0
1,1,1,1,1,1
0,1,1,1,0
1,0,0,0,1
0,0,0,0,1
0,0,1,1,0
0,0,0,0,1
1,0,0,0,1
0,1,1,1,0,1
0,0,0,1,0
0,1,0,1,0
0,1,0,1,0
0,1,0,1,0
0,1,1,1,1
0,0,0,1,0
0,0,0,1,0,1
4,8,9,15
0,0,0,0,0,0,0,0,1
0,0,0,0,0,0,0,0,0
1,0,0,0,0,1,0,0,1
```

```
1,0,0,0,0,1,0,0,1
0,1,0,0,1,0,0,1,0
0,1,0,0,1,0,0,1,0
0,0,1,1,0,0,1,0,0
0,0,1,1,1,1,1,0,0,1
0,0,0,1,1,0,0,0,0
0,0,1,0,0,0,0,0,0
0,0,1,1,1,1,1,0,0
0,0,0,0,0,0,1,0,0
0,0,0,0,0,1,0,0,0
0,0,0,0,1,0,0,0,0
0,0,0,1,0,0,0,0,0
0,0,0,1,0,0,0,0,0,1
0,0,0,0,0,0,0,0,0
0,0,0,0,0,0,0,0,0
0,0,0,1,1,1,0,0,0
0,0,0,0,0,1,0,0,0
0,0,0,0,0,1,0,0,0
0,0,0,0,0,1,0,0,0
0,0,0,0,0,1,0,0,0
0,0,0,0,0,1,0,0,0,1
0,0,0,0,0,0,0,0,0
0,1,0,0,0,0,0,0,0
0,0,1,1,1,1,1,0,0
0,0,1,0,0,0,0,1,0
0,0,1,0,0,0,0,1,0
0,0,1,0,0,0,0,1,0
0,0,1,0,0,0,0,1,0
0,0,1,1,1,1,1,1,0,1
4,7,6,25
1,1,1,1,0,0
1,0,0,0,1,0
1,0,0,0,1,0
1,0,0,0,1,0
1,1,1,1,0,0
1,0,0,0,0,0
1,0,0,0,0,0,1
0,0,0,0,0,0
0,0,0,0,0,0
0,1,1,1,0,0
1,0,0,0,1,0
1,1,1,1,0,0
1,0,0,0,0,0
0,1,1,1,0,0,1
```

```
0,0,0,0,0,0
0,0,0,0,0,0
0,1,1,1,0,0
0,0,0,0,1,0
0,1,1,1,1,0
1,0,0,0,1,0
0,1,1,1,0,1,1
0,0,0,0,0,0
0,0,0,0,0,0
0,0,1,1,1,0
0,1,0,0,0,0
0,1,0,0,0,0
0,1,0,0,0,0
0,0,1,1,1,0,1
0
```

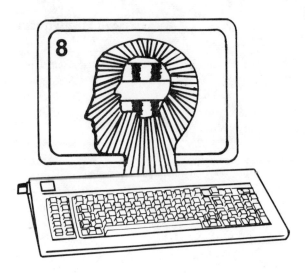

Expert Systems: Theory

Many people have heard the term *artificial intelligence*; most of those that have heard of AI will also have heard of *expert systems*. In fact, there are a significant number of people who have been introduced to artificial intelligence by way of expert systems.

As with artificial intelligence, there is a certain amount of disagreement as to what actually constitutes an expert system. Unlike AI, however, the notion of what an expert system ideally is, is reasonably well defined: an expert system is software designed to deliver the expertise of a human expert or group of human experts to other people (or other programs) who require expert advice. Expert systems are also known as consultative systems, and in some quarters it is argued that the term *decision support system* is just another euphemism for the same thing.

The reasons for constructing an expert system are varied, although most fall into one of several categories. The most obvious reason for building an expert system is that of distributing the knowledge of a human expert across an organization, so that their expertise can be utilized more efficiently by a larger group of people, ultimately at a reduced cost. Such systems may be used by other people or by computer programs that need to draw upon some "human" body of knowledge in order to perform their tasks.

A second use of expert systems, and one that is sometimes more palatable than the first, is that of providing training: since expert systems can be constructed to explain their reasoning process, such a system can be quite useful in situations where new employees, physicians, or other professionals are in need of the opportunity to test their knowledge in ways that are safe and replicable. In these situations, the trainee will be given some sort of a problem to solve and then approach the problem either on an independent basis with a follow-up by the expert system or in conjunction with the system from the beginning.

A third use of these programs is simply to serve as a repository of expert knowledge as a hedge against the expert leaving the company or retiring. There is usually an added benefit in constructing systems for this purpose: in being asked to "catalog" their expertise, people will often expand upon it, either through their own private reflection or through the interviewing that ultimately takes place as part of the system building process.

Finally, expert systems are used in circumstances in which the particular knowledge may not be particularly "expert," but the operating conditions are in some fashion not amendable to human presence, whether via some form of danger or hazardous conditions, or simply in the sense that the working conditions are likely to produce boredom or fatigue.

You will notice that these reasons for building expert systems roughly correspond to the arguments for using computers and then for using robots, as the history of information processing has demonstrated. It is in this sense that expert systems represent the latest effort in the evolution of the information society.

One can construct the components of a generic expert system without much difficulty: the *knowledge base*, the *inference engine*, and the *user interface*. Each of these areas is of critical concern in designing an expert system and will be addressed in turn.

Briefly, we can define the components as follows: the notion of a knowledge base has defined previously in this text as a storehouse of information, organized in some usable fashion. The inference engine is a set of strategies for using the knowledge in the knowledge base. Finally, the user interface is a collection of methods by which the program will interact with the end user. To be more specific, there must be an interface to the developer of the system, so that they may be certain that the system is functioning properly before releasing it to the end user. This interface may or may not be the same as the end user interface; usually, the end user interface will be a subset of the developer's interface. Therefore, we will consider the problems and issues of the user interface to encompass both the developer's and the end user's interface to the system.

An expert system also should have a number of features, or characteristics, which again have an important impact on its design. These characteristics will serve two purposes: to make the expert system function better and to improve its acceptance by the end user.

The first of these characteristics is that the system should be able to *explain* its reasoning process, both during the process of a consultation and at its end. The notion here is that the user should be able to answer the question: "Why are you asking me this question now?" during the consultation, and "How is it that you came to that conclusion?" at the end. Responses from the system will take the general form of "Since you have told me that X, Y and Z are true, then I am pursuing the possibility (or was able to establish) that A may be (or was) true as well."

The reason for the desirability of this attribute is twofold: one, the developer of the system must be able to check its process during a consultation, and two, people are unwilling to take any advice (generally speaking) unless they can establish that the advice giver has some rationale for giving that particular advice. This is particularly the case (as it has been shown) with expert systems: the system must be able to justify its advice in as explicitly a fashion as possible if there is to be any likelihood of the end user taking the advice generated.

Another attribute is that the expert system must be able to ask questions in a manner that makes the most efficient use of the end user's time: in other words, if there is sufficient evidence to rule out one hypothesis, the system should not continue to ask questions about it. For example, consider a medical expert system whose purpose is to give assistance in diagnosing emergency room patient complaints. If a patient came in with a sharp pain in his or her side following a traffic accident, you would not expect that the first questions would center around the history of cancer in the patient's family; although that certainly could be an explanation for their pain, however unlikely. Instead, the system should inquire about the accident, trying to determine if that side of the patient was struck or wrenched during the accident, this being the most likely explanation for the source of the pain.

This feature will again serve two purposes: first of all, it should make the consultation more efficient, as only questions with a high degree of plausibility will be asked at any given time. Secondly, such a style of questioning will make the system appear to be more "rational" to the end user, and this will probably contribute to their cooperation during the consultation, as well as their likelihood of following the advice given later.

Following this theme, there should be an easy way for the system to accept data that it has not explicitly asked for, either as a way of initializing the system or as a way of allowing the user to input data that may not have been directly requested by the system. Again, the parallels to a human consultation here should be clear: often, the person seeking advice will want to describe the initial situation before being asked specific questions; similarly, they may have some information "jogged" to consciousness in an unpredictable manner that suddenly needs the attention of the expert.

Finally, an ideal expert system would not simply be a static system, but instead would be able to modify its knowledge base over time, either as a result of feedback from the consultative sessions or as a result of new information that had suddenly come to light and needed to be integrated into the knowledge base. It should be noted, however, that this is not as critical a component as the other attributes: it is entirely reasonable to construct an expert system for use in such a manner that its knowledge base is relatively static. Such examples might involve a system that establishes the viability of a potential mortgage client: while the data items such as available capital in the lending institution, interest rates, and so on might change, the overall logic would remain reasonably stable. This can be seen in contrast to a legal system in which the knowledge base might be so dynamic that the advice given would shift dramatically over the course of time, based in part on how successful the advice given previously had been.

To summarize: an expert system is a computer system used to distribute the expertise of a human or group of humans throughout a group of users that might otherwise not have access to that expertise. They can be seen as having three component subsystems: the knowledge base, the inference engine, and the user interface.

Characteristically, successful expert systems have the capability to explain their reasoning process, ask the questions that are most pertinent given the information received from the end user, and accept data in batches that supercede the interactive process. Some advanced expert systems have the ability to "learn" from their interactions or otherwise expand on their knowledge base in a dynamic manner.

The area that the system is designed to be an "expert" in is referred to as the *domain*, and the human expert is known as the *domain expert*. Typically, there is at least one *knowledge engineer* or senior programmer with the responsibility of building the expert system, as well as of extracting the expertise from the domain expert.

As a contrast to the generic system described above, it is interesting to consider the first diagnostic system that was developed for medical purposes. It had goals somewhat similar to those mentioned above, in that it attempted to provide a mechanical version of human expertise; however, it operated purely on statistics, with some fascinating results.

In statistics, there is a type of analysis known as *clustering*. For example, the high temperatures on a group of summer days will cluster together at a higher set of values than those for winter. Now if we took those data and combined them with the percentage of time that the sky was clear, we might see more refined clusters developing the highest temperatures, high percentages of clear skies, and summer dates; perhaps the lowest temperatures, high percentages of clear skies, and summer dates; perhaps the lowest temperatures, high percentages of clear skies, and winter temperatures (due to radiational cooling); and so on. The notion here is that clusters of data will most likely represent different phenomena, although no guarantee of this is given; it is just a statistical likelihood.

Now in this medical system, a group of patients was selected, with the characteristics that each had one of four diseases that had been diagnosed by their physicians. Each of the patients was subjected to a battery of tests, without any knowledge or presumption that the tests performed had anything to do in particular with the disease that they had been diagnosed as having. The data generated from these tests was collected and subjected to cluster analysis. If the hypothesis that people with the same disease should generate similar test results held true, then the final results would show four clusters, each corresponding to one of the four disease groups.

In fact, five clusters were discovered: four of the clusters corresponded to the four disease categories, but the fifth had patients from a variety of the four groups. At first this was a disappointment, as it seemed as though it would be impossible to discover which tests had led most efficiently to discovering which diseases; however, on a hunch the researchers had physicians reexamine the patients more closely, and they discovered that the fifth group had actually been misdiagnosed and that they all shared a common disease.

Now, this was not a good example of artificial intelligence; it was, instead, a good example of the power of statistical analysis. Nonetheless, it does raise the issue of what constitutes an expert system: is predicting the outcome of certain tests sufficient, even though there is no "intelligence" (as commonly understood) involved, just *brute force*? If this is not considered to be a worthwhile goal, on the other hand, what is? These are questions that researchers must ultimately answer on a pragmatic basis.

KNOWLEDGE ACQUISITION:

One of the central issues facing that of expert system design is the question of how the expertise is to be acquired, or *extracted*, from the human experts. This also raises the more detailed issue of the source of the expertise, which is not always restricted to human experts. Other sources of expertise can be manuals, texts, and other documents; computer-generated data, along with some statistical analyses of these data; and computer-generated expertise through systems that are designed to simulate the area of investigation and/or learn from experience with the actual area or a simulation of it.

The question of how the knowledge is to be acquired is intimately tied to the approach that is going to be used for representing the knowledge in the expert system. Without realizing it, knowledge engineers can embark on the design of an expert system that is fated to be constricted by the knowledge representation scheme chosen, in ways that are not immediately apparent. This will be not simply because some types of knowledge are more easily represented in one form than they are in another: the structure that the knowledge is ultimately to take colors the knowledge acquisition process in ways that neither the knowledge engineer nor the domain expert is likely to be aware of.

KNOWLEDGE REPRESENTATION SCHEMES:

There are two general classes of expert systems as characterized by their knowledge representation schemes: *rule-based* and *frame-based*. Additionally, there has been a third category proposed: that of the hybrid system, which makes use of both rules and frames for the representation of knowledge. Most frame-based systems, however, make use of rules, so we shall consider only the first two categories in this discussion.

Recently, there have emerged a variety of products on the market that have become known as expert system *shells*, or tools for building expert systems. At a minimum, they provide the knowledge engineer with a computer language that is tailored to the problems of knowledge representation and/or expert systems in general. Most will also include programming tools for managing the user interface through the construction of menus and the testing of responses for validity in terms of range, type, and so on, and perhaps a graphics interface as well. Other facilities provided by some shells include the ability to "discover" rules from a set of examples by a mathematical process known as *induction*, interfaces to computerized data and other computer programs, and the graphic representation of the knowledge base itself, to mention a few.

THE INFERENCE ENGINE:

The structure of the inference engine is an expert system is one of critical concern. It is the task of the inference engine to operate on the knowledge base in such a manner that the knowledge represented there is accessed not only efficiently, but consistently. There are two levels at which the inference engine can be viewed; we can concentrate on either the forms of logic the engine uses or the manner in which the rules and/or frames are processed.

Earlier in this text, we reviewed the usefulness of fuzzy logic as compared to classic logic. As a review, fuzzy logic is applicable when intermediate values between true and false are desired; for example, fuzzy logic would be used if the knowledge engineer did not want to insist that the end user have to reply either yes or no to the question "Is it raining outside?"

In expert systems, the end user is often in a situation in which his or her knowledge of the condition is vague and/or imprecise; in fact, it is probably due to this state of affairs that they have a need to consult an expert. Likewise, the tendency of domain experts is to express their own reasoning process in similarly vague (or intuitive) terms it is thus desirable to be able to express their expertise in a manner that does not force precision where it is not useful. Thus, the use of fuzzy logic can often be central to the success of an expert system's functioning.

Another reasoning process that is quite useful in the domain of expert systems is that of *Bayesian inference*. Bayesian inference is a mathematical method for processing probability factors in such a manner that successive values can yield an overall probability factor that is consistent with reality. Probability values, like fuzzy logic values, range between 0.0 and 1.0, but are processed differently. Let us take the example of the function AND. In fuzzy logic, when two values are combined through the AND operation, the minimum value is used as the result. In probability theory, which is a more general case of Bayesian inference, the values would be multiplied. Using the following assignments, we can construct the fuzzy logic phrases and results of their combination via AND:

A = Jane is smart = 0.90
B = Jane is tall = 0.90

The fuzzy logic phrasing of the two values would be:

Jane is very smart; Jane is very tall.

In probability theory, we would instead say:

There is a 90 percent chance that Jane is smart; there is a 90 percent chance that Jane is tall.

Notice that in probability theory there is no question as to being "somewhat" tall, "very" tall, or anything similar. Instead, Jane is either tall or she is not tall; it is just that we have (in this particular example) a 90 percent chance of knowing whether she is tall or not. In fuzzy logic, by contrast, Jane is not simply tall or not tall, but she can be varying degrees of tall.

Now, to take the AND function (A AND B), we would produce the following values:

```
Fuzzy Logic:    A AND B = MINIMUM (A, B)
                        = MINIMUM (0.90, 0.90)
                        = 0.90

Probability:    A AND B = A * B
                        = 0.90 * 0.90
                        = 0.81
```

The phrases corresponding to A AND B are:

fuzzy logic: Jane is very much of a smart, tall person.

Probability: There is an 81 percent chance that Jane is both smart and tall.

Now, there are cases where the use of fuzzy logic (such as the above example) is the preferred manner of processing the knowledge at hand, and others (such as the calculation of how certain an end user is about a given set of conditions) where probability theory is best suited. As an example of the latter, if there were five on/off conditions, each of which were 90 percent certain to be on, it would be better to indicate that there was 59 percent chance that they were all on, rather than to use the fuzzy logic that says that as a group they are were "very" on.

A robust expert system, then, will make use of both fuzzy logic and Bayesian inference in its inference engine, to allow for the broadest use of available knowledge.

At the other end of the spectrum, in the case of rule-based systems, is the question of whether the system is restricted to backward chaining or has the flexibility to perform forward chaining as well. While a system, could be written without the use of forward chaining, it would be quite cumbersome and would often either ask questions that were not relevant or have to go through complicated hoops to avoid asking those questions.

To understand the difference between backward and forward chaining, let us construct a rudimentary expert system for medical diagnosis. This system can be represented as a graph when forward chaining is available and as a tree when forward chaining is not available. Let us proceed with a system that is restricted to backward chaining, and then add the capability of forward chaining.

At the root of our tree will be a null node, serving as a place holder. Immediately below that node will be a set of nodes that represent the ultimate diagnosis to be delivered; one and only one of these nodes will be chosen as the best as a result of the consultation.

Beneath each of these nodes, their children will be the most general level of symptoms that could lead to each diagnosis. For example, if the diagnosis was measles, it could have children of the sort "patient has spots," "patient has not had measles before," "patient has an elevated temperature," and so on. This would be the level that most domain experts could express the most easily.

Each of these children could be parents to another set of nodes, which would in turn specify more explicitly the knowledge obtained. Thus, the statement "patient has elevated temperature" could have the children "patient is a child AND temperature is greater than 101 degrees," and "patient is an adult AND temperature is greater than 99.5 degrees." This would continue perhaps one level deeper to establish the patient's age, with nodes that equate ages with either childhood or adulthood.

Notice, that this example is a good candidate for fuzzy logic: the phrase

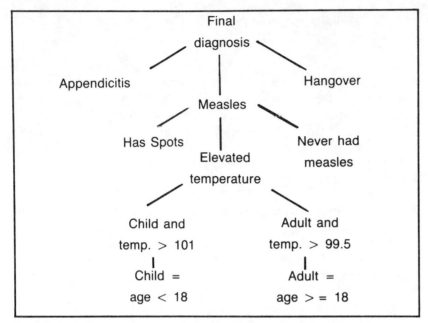

Fig. 8-1. Part of a tree for a resolve expert system for medical diagnosis.

"has an elevated temperature" is a fuzzy phrase, and could be determined by a fuzzy rule, such as "a patient's temperature is elevated to the degree that they are young and it is very high, or that they are not young and it is more or less high." Fuzzy logic would allow the age at which a child becomes an adult to be imprecise and would further allow the definition of what is a high temperature to be expressed as a dynamic range, rather than simply over or under a particular value.

Notice in the tree in Fig. 9-1 that there are three possible diagnoses; appendicitis, measles, and hangover. We have only drawn the children of the measles node for the time being, and will explore the other nodes later. Let us consider now how the expert system would operate in a backwards chaining mode.

The primary concept is that a node can be *resolved* by assigning a value to it. This value can be generated either by asking the user for data or by operating on data that is available internally to that node; in this case the data is available exclusively from its children. If a node is unresolved, the system will try to resolve that node by examining its children. If it finds that the children have resolved values, then it will use those values to try to resolve the parent node; otherwise, it will recursively try to resolve those children, and so on.

A node will actually consist of one of the following generic types of information:

1. The node will contain a pure value and will be resolved. A node of this type, whose purpose would be to state that the average body temperature is 98.6 degrees fahrenheit, might be:

AVERAGE = 98.6

2. The node will contain a potential value that can be resolved by asking the user for the actual value. This type of node would look something like:

> OBTAIN TEMPERATURE USING "What is the patient's temperature?"

3. The node will contain a potential value to be calculated by operations on data already supplied via steps (1) and (2). For example:

FEVER = TEMPERATURE – AVERAGE

This last category can be more than a simple calculation; in the example used earlier, the rule might be:

> IF (TEMPERATURE > 101.0) AND (AGE < 16) THEN FEVER = TRUE

Let us generate a portion of a simple expert system to discover that the patient has measles via backwards chaining. First we will presume that the system, like human doctors, collects certain information as a matter of course, independent of the particular problem. In our case, this will mean that the patient's age and temperature have already been obtained. (The reason for this method will become clear).

```
Name:       ROOT
Parent:     None
Children:   MEASLES, APPENDICITIS, HANGOVER
Rule:       PRINT "You have the following disease:"
            PRINT DIAGNOSIS

Name:       MEASLES
Parent:     ROOT
Children:   SPOTS, FEVER, HAD_BEFORE
Rule:       IF (SPOTS = TRUE) AND
               (FEVER = TRUE) AND
               (HAD_BEFORE = FALSE)
```

```
                THEN
                    DIAGNOSIS = "Measles"

Name:           SPOTS
Parent:         MEASLES
Children:       None
Rule:           OBTAIN SPOTS (YESNO) USING
                    "Do you have red spots all over your body?"


Name:           FEVER
Parent:         MEASLES
Children:       AGE_TYPE
Rule:           IF ((AGE_TYPE = ADULT) AND (TEMPERATURE > 99.5))
                    OR
                    ((AGE_TYPE = CHILD) AND (TEMPERATURE > 101.0))
                THEN
                    FEVER = TRUE


Name:           AGE_TYPE
Parent:         FEVER
Children:       None
Rule:           IF (AGE > 16)
                THEN
                    AGE_TYPE = ADULT
                OTHERWISE
                    AGE_TYPE = CHILD

Name:           HAD_BEFORE
Parent:         MEASLES
Children:       None
Rule:           OBTAIN HAD_BEFORE (YESNO) USING
                    "Have you had measles before?"
```

The processing of this system would proceed, in a backwards chaining model, as follows: the system (having obtained the age and temperature of the patient), would then attempt to resolve the root node. Let us assume that the patient's age is 12 and the temperature is 102.5.

Encountering the variable DIAGNOSIS, it would find that it had not been assigned a value, and would try and resolve a value for it. By some method—whether it be leftmost child, or "best" child first, a function of the inference engine—it moves to that child, in this case, MEASLES. Here is finds three variables, all without any assigned values; SPOTS, FEVER, and HAD__BEFORE. Before it can decide on whether to pass "Measles" up to the root, it must evaluate these three items.

It first goes to SPOTS, and discovers that it has an "askable" node: in other words, it must prompt the user for the value required. When it asks if he or she has red spots all over the body, it receives a YES answer and passes the value TRUE up to the node MEASLES.

It then proceeds with the next child, FEVER. In the FEVER node it finds a rule that requires two values: AGE__TYPE and TEMPERATURE. Since it encounters AGE__TYPE first, it discovers that it has no value assigned to it, and proceeds downward to the node AGE__TYPE. Here it performs a calculation based on data that it already has—the patient's age—and passes the value up to its parent, FEVER. Since the patient is age 12, this value is CHILD.

Back in the FEVER node, the system takes the value CHILD for AGE__TYPE and 102.5 for TEMPERATURE and discovers that FEVER = TRUE, which it passes up to MEASLES. Now the system takes the last child, HAD__BEFORE, and asks the user if he or she has had measles before. The response is NO, and so the value FALSE is assigned to HAD__BEFORE and passed up to MEASLES.

Finally, all the variables have been resolved, and the system can evaluate the rule in MEASLES. It finds that all the values match, and so passes "Measles" up to DIAGNOSIS. DIAGNOSIS, now having received a value for itself, prints the message out to the user and terminates.

There are several problems that present themselves with this approach, and they will serve to illustrate the issues of expert system design. First, let us consider the node AGE__TYPE. It is likely that this information could be useful in more diagnoses than MEASLES, but it is resolved in this model as a result of pursuing the MEASLES branch. Does this mean that the node should be duplicated in other branches? Or should it be resolved in the beginning, before the system starts down the tree (as we did with AGE and TEMPERATURE)? Or perhaps we should allow AGE__TYPE to have more than one parent, in which case it will be necessary to design the system so that it knows which parent it will have to return to, once it has resolved the AGE__TYPE node. These are all alternatives that have been used in one expert system or another, and they each have their advantages and disadvantages. The important issue here is that the decisions we make about this problem will have a direct impact on the structure of the knowledge base and the functioning of the inference engine, and because of this, such decisions are critical to the design of the expert system overall.

Another issue glossed over in this review was what happens if the criteria for a diagnosis of MEASLES were not achieved. In this case, the MEASLES node would have to have some way of passing control over to the next diagnosis, again an issue for the inference engine. Options here, alluded to earlier, are to proceed from one diagnostic branch to the next simply on the basis of the order in which they appear in the knowledge base or to use some sort of ordering function so that the most likely diagnosis is investigated first. Again, the answers to these concerns have everything to do with the design of the knowledge and inference engine.

Another problem is that of unknown data: it is often the case that the user will not know the answer to a question. For example, when asked if he or she has had measles before, a reasonable response would be "I don't know." And while some systems can afford the luxury of insisting that the user go out and find the answer before proceeding, more often this will not be possible or desirable. In these cases the knowledge engineer will have to have prepared rules for handling responses of the type UNKNOWN. Some expert systems will "propagate" the UNKNOWN value as far up the tree as possible; others will insist on its resolution as soon as it is received, by either assigning a default value to the variable or taking some other predetermined action.

An issue more mundane than the previous ones, but important nonetheless, is the checking that must go into any responses received from the user. Some of these checks can simply be *true* checks that do not allow numeric responses to yes/no questions or textural responses to numeric requests, and so on. Other fruitful types of checking include *range* checking: for example, if a patient responds with 986 when asked for his temperature, this is obviously not a correct response. Will the system simply ask for another response, or will it contain some "intelligence" about possible causes for the error (that is, a missing decimal point)? Such matters are not new to the field of data processing, but they are even more critical when it comes to a highly interactive system such as this.

As a final consideration, there is the issue of how the conclusions are presented to the user. While this might at first glance appear to be even more mundane than the previous issue, it can be so serious an obstacle that results will be ignored or not believed if it is handled improperly.

One of the first expert systems was a medical expert system for diagnosing infections. It led the way to a cornucopia of medical expert systems, but all met with serious resistance from the majority of physicians. The reason appears to have been that the results were presented as facts: "The patient has measles," or "Perform an appendectomy immediately." What these systems failed to take into consideration was the position of a physician in the medical community (not to mention the larger community) as an expert upon whose shoulders falls a tremendous amount of responsibility. Using a computer to perform a task—diagnosis, which is felt to be one of the most challenging tasks a physician can face—threw the quantlet down squarely at the physician. As a result, most would refuse to use such a system at best, or at worst they would not accept is conclusions if they disagreed with their own.

The resolution of this dilemma was to first of all recall that no computer program would be given the responsibility assigned to a human physician; ultimately, it could only be a tool in their diagnostic repertoire. Secondly, it had to assume the position that the physician to have more information available to them, and if the program were consulted privately, no one would have to know what the actual outcome of the consultation was. Finally, the manner in which the program would interact would be to ask the physician for the facts of a particular case and the diagnosis that the physician and arrived at. The system would then calculate its own diagnosis and report the results to the physician in the terms alluded to: either the diagnoses agreed, in which case the system reported that it had been successful in its attempts to learn from the physician, or they disagreed, in which case the system would ask for further instruction so that it could understand where it went wrong.

While this last part might appear to be a bit convoluted, there is actually a good reason (beyond getting the physician to listen to the system) for presenting the results this way. If one views the ultimate goal of the expert system to be that of improving the quality of medical care, we must evaluate this strategy in those terms. Now, it is a well-established fact that people have an increased capacity for learning new things when they are asked to describe the differences between situations, objects, or whatever. By asking the physicians to describe the differences between the system's diagnosis and their own, the expert system was creating an environment that stood the best chance possible of enhancing the physician's medical expertise. As a bonus, this also presented the expert system with the opportunity to expand and refine its own knowledge base. Thus, a certain amount of diplomacy served all parties well. Such will often be the case when using expert systems.

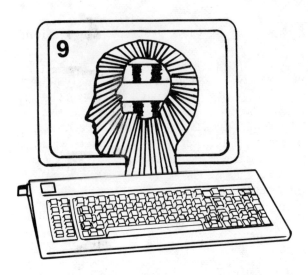

Expert Systems:

Applications

In the previous chapter we examined some of the qualities of expert systems and the broad issues associated with their design. In this chapter we will explore working expert systems, the more detailed issues that must be addressed during their design, and the tools used in their development. Our purpose will be to determine what expert systems can and cannot do, and what are reasonable expectations of the efforts involved in developing such a system.

In an attempt to understand the problems involved in expert system design, construction, and use, we must first develop an appreciation of the computer and human systems that interact to produce and use an expert system.

The primary program components of an expert system, as outlined previously, are the knowledge base, the inference engine, and the man-machine interface. There are also three groups of people involved in the design of expert systems: the expert, the knowledge engineer, and the user. There are, of course, some uncommon systems in which the user and/or the expert are not people but are instead either mechanical systems or textual experts, but in any event the same types of systems will need to be considered.

DEVELOPING AN EXPERT SYSTEM

Before an expert system can be designed, there are a number of critical questions that must be answered. The first is to make an initial decision concerning what the domain of expertise will be: is this is a system that will deal with knowledge about cars, medicine, or world politics? While this may appear to be an obvious decision, it is one that usually becomes much less trivial than originally anticipated. Determining the boundaries of what is to be part of the expert system's domain and what is not is quite often a grueling and potentially heated endeavor.

The Purpose of the System

The next task is to determine to what use the expert system will be put. Again, while this appears to be a simple question, the generation of a precise answer to it is critical to the success of the final product. While there may be a great deal of initial agreement as to what the purpose of the system should be, the refinement of the answer to this will involve a detailed assessment of the method of knowledge acquisition to be used, the type of user the system is intended for, and so on. As a guide, it is worth considering the general classes of expert systems in the world today.

There are four basic purposes for which an expert system can be used each with its own requirements, difficulties, and advantages. The most common application of expert systems is for the purpose originally devised: to deliver expertise, usually human, to a large number of users who would not otherwise have access to that human expert or experts. But this, while it is the most obvious reason for building an expert system, is far from the only purpose to which they can be applied.

A second, major type of expert-system application is that of training human users in a field that is unfamiliar to them by providing them with an opportunity to match their skills against an expert, albeit a mechanical one. Furthermore, since this expert will have the ability to tirelessly explain itself, offer suggestions and advice, and respond to a large number of variations on the same theme, the computerized expert makes for an excellent teacher's aide.

Expert systems are also able to be used as a dynamic archive of knowledge, as opposed to simply a static, encyclopedic reference. By allowing the user to interact with the system rather than simply look up portions of text, the user is able to gain a richer understanding of the subject matter, and will in all likelihood be able to both retain and use the information for a much longer period of time.

Finally, expert systems can be used to exert control in situations that people would normally find to be intolerable due to the high volume of data to be assimilated, the hazardous conditions under which the controller must be present, or the tediousness or tiresomeness of the situation itself, which would reduce a person's ability to remain alert and effective.

Each of these sets of circumstances makes a particular set of demands upon the expert system, and thus results in what are ultimately very different approaches to expert systems. While it may be arguable at one level that each system will simply be a method of allowing a person to interrogate a knowledge base and receive conclusions as a result, the fabric of these systems is quite different when viewed at a closer level. For example, note the contrast between the "classic" expert system—the one that delivers advice to the user in need of a consultation—and the training system. In the first system, the emphasis on delivering explanations, the facility for trying out different sets of responses, and the overall "chattiness" of the system will be features kept at a minimum, as compared to that of the training system, which must be prepared to go into more detail and afford the user a large set of alternative examples. Such seemingly superficial differences will have a major impact on the architecture of the actual expert system.

Who Will The User Be?

During the complete life cycle of expert system development, it is crucial to consider the end user and what his or her characteristics will be. There are a number of spectra across which the user may range, and the characteristics of each of these ranges will have a significant impact on the "flavor" of the final system.

One of the first things to establish is whether the user will be a person, another computer system, or some combination of the two. If the user is "simply" another computer system, the question of the user interface is somewhat simplified, although it is highly unlikely that an expert system would interact purely with another computer or set of machinery. Therefore, the extent to which the expert system must interact with people and how much of that interaction will involve other machines must be clearly delineated at the outset of the design process.

Presuming that the primary users are people, the first question that must be asked is how much expertise do they have in the domain itself, and consequently, how much direct access will they have to the knowledge base and inferencing mechanisms. It will be safer in many respects if the users are restricted from these subsystems, no matter what their levels of knowledge about the domain are. It may, however, occasionally be useful to allow the user to interact with the expert system at a more fundamental level for the purposes of expanding the knowledge base through direct interaction with and intervention from the user.

Also of critical importance in the initial stages is to assess what level of competence the user has with the computer system they will be using the expert system on. The less competent the user, the richer the man-machine interface will have to be, although this is no excuse for an overly sparse interface simply because the users are technically astute.

Related to the above issue are the two issues of reward and threat that are well-known to traditional systems analysts. The user may experience the expert system as a boon, a threat, or (rarely) a neutral influence on their lives; a complete analysis of the potential benefits and the obstacles to implementing this system will be critical if the system is ever to get beyond being yet another clever tool and achieve true usefulness. Again, these two scales, threat and benefit, must be assessed independently, as it is not at all unlikely that a single user could perceive a new system as being both quite threatening and potentially quite useful.

Domain Selection

During the final selection of the domain for the expert system, careful attention must be paid to its definition: the more clearly that the domain is defined, the easier the job of building the expert system will be. In attempting to clarify the domain definition, some guidelines are useful:

1. Is there a recognized expert (or group of experts) available? How long will that expert be available: just during the initial phases or throughout the development life cycle? Many times a development group will attempt to build a system with less than complete domain expertise available and find themselves with a system that either doesn't work at all or is, at best, trivial.

2. As stated previously, are there clear boundaries around the domain? When building a medical system, for example, it is important to clearly define which specialty of medicine will be addressed and to do so as precisely as possible. In the MYCIN system, the domain was strictly limited to a class of blood diseases, and as such it has been a successful system; however, were the system to be asked about broken arms, appendicitis, or even other systemic infections, MYCIN would be no more useful than a payroll program. When the limits of the domain are known, the expert system can be finite and therefore finished.

3. Are the objectives of the system well defined? Beyond simply defining the domain, it must be clear what the purposes of the system are: will it be used for training, issuing advice, or controlling some real-time robotic system? Will the system have to do a lot of textual processing as part of its input and output? To what extent will graphics be used, and to what purpose? All these are critical questions, as they will determine the underlying "flavor" of the system.

4. Is the expertise under question capable of being represented in either rules or frames, and within a reasonable period of time? Some domains require so much work to represent in a structured format that the feasibility of building the system must be called into question; if at all possible, this should be determined at the very beginning of the project, before major commitments to the development process are made.

5. Is the expertise fundamentally dependent upon understanding, as opposed to common sense? This is really a variation upon the concept in number four above, and it represents the core of difficulty when it comes

to building expert systems. What is often apparent to people is not immediately reducible to a series of structured statements and thus is not a reasonable candidate for an expert system. For example, when hammering a nail, the placing of the pointed end of the nail against the wood, the holding of the hammer at the end of the handle furthest from the head, and the use of the flat end of the head rather than the claw are all examples of the common sense knowledge of carpenters. If asked, a carpenter could easily explain the rationale for doing these things, but such an explanation would almost certainly not be included in a description of how to build cabinets. Despite the fact that the relationship of a hammer and a nail is obvious, it actually incorporates a rather sophisticated network of understanding relative to the use of tools, physics, and safety, which would take a tremendous amount of code to establish. Therefore, if the expert system is highly dependent upon the establishment of such knowledge, it will quickly become too large and unwieldy to implement.

6. Finally, are the benefits to the use of the system clear to all involved? A system that is quite clever, from a knowledge engineer's point of view, may be either too expensive to design and implement or too threatening to the end user.

Information Sources

When the expert system is up and running, what will the sources of information to the system be? Will the system simply interact with the user, or will there be other sources of information that the expert system uses to help it render its advice? The most common alternative sources of information are the following:

Online/Static. There is frequently a database of information that a commercial expert system makes reference to in the course of its consultation. This database may reflect current inventories, prices, territories, and so on. This type of information is largely unchanged by the consultation with the expert system and exists primarily as an archive for use by the system. This type of resource is easily incorporated into expert systems and does not usually represent a drain on the resources of the overall computer system when the expert system is in use. A typical expert system that uses this type of information source would be a system designed to schedule shipment of parts between warehouses and factory sites.

Online/Dynamic. In this case, the information is still resident on the overall computer system, but it will either be changed as a result of the consultation with the expert system or be a type of information that is itself dynamic. Again, the typical structure of this information will be a database, but in this case it may be either updated by the expert system or updated on some regular basis by another set of processes. An example of a system that might interact with this type of information source is a network advisor that gives advice as to the best way of adding terminals to a computer system on a temporary basis. The information source in this case would be updated by the number of locations that were currently online, but a strictly "real-time" basis would not be used. These types of information sources are similar to the static sources in the ease with which they can be accessed by the expert system, but they do represent a greater drain on system resources, since issues of distributed processing, data integrity, and so on must be dealt with.

Real Time. Data of this sort is the most difficult to capture and process in an expert system, since the time of its input is critical in determining not only its usefulness but its validity. As in traditional programming, real time systems represent the greatest challenge to system developers. In the case of expert systems, this difficulty is exaggerated, since most expert system development tools are more interested in the delivery of good advice, rather than timely advice. Thus real-time expert systems will invariably have to be written "from scratch," thereby exposing the systems to all the potential problems involved with reinventing the wheel. Nonetheless, such systems have been built, including a system which acts as an assistant to air traffic controllers.

Development Stages

The expert system development team must decide upon its membership and the time frames during which each of those members will be present. In order to assess this question completely, it will be useful to consider various stages of expert system development:

Domain Selection. The user, expert, and knowledge engineer convene to decide upon the desired limits of the expert system. This process should yield (ideally) a written definition of the domain to be encoded.

System Design. The type of knowledge representation scheme is chosen, the man-machine interface is described, and so on. Again the user, expert, and knowledge engineer are involved in this process. At the end of this stage, a written model of the expert system is complete.

Knowledge Acquisition. The knowledge engineer and expert work to extract as much of the knowledge as possible, using interviews with typical users wherever possible. The goal of this stage is to have a reasonably complete knowledge base.

Initial Prototyping. The knowledge engineer works to develop a first pass at the expert system that will embody the general format of the system and contain a representative portion of the knowledge processing that is intended for the final product. This will then be reviewed by the user and expert for consistency, and work will proceed into the next stage.

Final Prototyping. The knowledge engineer completes the expert system to the point that the entire knowledge base is available to the system, and the man-machine interface is largely complete. At the end of this phase a copy of the system is delivered to the users for their comments and criticisms.

Tuning. The knowledge engineer, working most closely with the user but in consultation with the expert if at all possible, puts the finishing touches on the system, a process that is always in danger of becoming infinite in length. It is at this stage that a clear definition of the domain and purposes of the system becomes critical.

DEVELOPMENT TOOLS

As mentioned earlier, there are a number of development tools that are available to the expert system developer in the form of expert system *shells* as well as in the form of advanced languages. We will consider some of the advantages and disadvantages of these tools and then examine a set typical systems built using the various approaches described.

The notion of an expert system shell is a straightforward one: instead of having to generate a new expert system every time one is required, a shell allows the developer to develop the inference engine, user interface, and structure of the knowledge base once, in a manner that is independent of the domain. Following this, "all" that remains to be accomplished is the knowledge acquisition process, encoding that knowledge in the proper form, and prototyping the system. In the case of commercially available shells, this means that the system developer purchases a shell, uses the strategies of the shell's developers for knowledge representation, and implements the system. Such shells can range in price from several hundred dollars (for microcomputers) to several tens of thousand (for special hardware systems).

Advantages of Shells

The primary advantage of an expert system shell is that of reduced development time (and cost). This advantage is the result of a number of factors including the following:

An established knowledge representation scheme. Integral to the shell will be a well-developed scheme that will serve as a structure for the knowledge acquisition and encoding processes. At one level, a great deal of development effort is saved by using an established scheme, since this often represents one of the most difficult conceptual tasks of the development itself. Beyond this advantage, it is also the case that by familiarizing oneself with the knowledge representation scheme of a shell, the knowledge engineer can more easily conduct the knowledge acquisition process and more quickly render the acquired knowledge into a usable format. This area is probably the one in which the most dramatic savings are to be found.

Established debugging facilities. A good shell will have built into it a broad range of facilities for testing the system. These facilities will in some respects be the same in principle as the ones used to help the user understand the reasoning process the system is pursuing, but they will also include some or all of the following: a *trace* facility for investigating in greater detail the process by which the system arrived at its conclusions; a *factors* facility for dynamically investigating the state of the expert system during its use; the ability to force immediate and/or intermediate conclusions; the ability to consider new data, forget old data, and/or change facts already established. Finally, some form of *save* facility will almost certainly be included, so that the entire consultation in any given state of completion can be saved and restarted at a later date. All these features represent a great deal of design effort, and having them immediately available will be of significant value to the knowledge engineer.

Fewer "nitty gritty" experts required. When building an expert system from scratch, there is a need for highly competent systems experts whose responsibilities will include the design, debugging, and maintenance of the components of the expert system that would otherwise be provided by the shell. Such professionals will be less likely to have the skills required for the knowledge acquisition process, which presents a subtle difficulty: when the system is built with a shell, there is typically only one person-to-person interface: the expert to the knowledge engineer. In the case of a system developed from scratch, there will now be another interface, that of the knowledge engineer to the system engineer, who will be unlikely to interact directly with the expert. This complicates the implementation of the expert system measurably and may well introduce shortcomings or inaccuracies into the final system. In any event, by enlarging the system that must be built to include the shell's components, the staff required to produce the final system must ultimately increase.

Prototyping encouraged at a higher level. Since the shell will provide a ready-made inference engine, knowledge representation scheme, and man-machine interface, it will not be necessary to experiment with different approaches to these problems. Instead, the knowledge engineer can concentrate on how to implement the knowledge of the expert, and experiment with the various logical paths that a consultation will invariably follow. Since changes that are found to be necessary will not require changing any of the integral structures of the shell, the prototyping also becomes more rapid and efficient.

Disadvantages of Shells

With any decision, there are always trade offs between advantages and disadvantages, and it is usually the case that the positive aspects of one side reflect hidden negative aspects. The choice of whether to use a shell or not is no exception: there are a number of reasons *not* to use a shell:

A restricted knowledge representation scheme. By choosing to use someone else's approach to knowledge representation, the knowledge engineer "buys" the limits of that approach, many of which may not be recognized by the engineer. For example, should a particular shell not offer the automatic use of arrays and tables, this will make it more difficult to accept, process, and deliver information in tabular form. The immediate consequence is clear: such requirements will require greater time and effort on the part of the knowledge engineer, and if the domain is such that arrays and tables are particularly useful, then there will be an increase in the cost of developing the system via that shell. A more subtle impact arises without any of the personnel involved necessarily being aware of it, an impact that can, if conditions are "right," have a tremendously negative effect on the final expert system: the knowledge engineer, finding tables difficult, will naturally and often unconsciously either find ways to get around having to use them or, worse yet, not extract knowledge that is dependent upon them. This does not happen simply because the use of tables requires a greater effort: it is due to the fact that, if a person is working with a given cognitive model of a knowledge representation system, it will be highly unlikely that they will even recognize aspects of the knowledge base that do not correspond to the structure of that knowledge representation scheme. This is an unavoidable problem, inherent in all expert systems, whether or not they are developed through the use of a shell. It is, however, exacerbated in those systems that use a "canned" knowledge representation scheme, since such schemes must ultimately strive for generality instead of the specificity that would be tailored to the particular domain, user, and expert in question.

Restricted debugging facilities. The fact that a particular developer imagined that a set of debugging aids would be useful does not imply that these tools will in all cases correspond to the facilities a given knowledge engineer will require. Furthermore, the types of debugging that will be possible when working with a shell will be limited by the features of the shell as well as by the fact that the shell itself will be proprietary (presuming that it is a commercial shell) and as such not directly accessible. These problems should be of relatively minor concern in a well-constructed shell, but they are of critical concern when deciding upon a particular shell.

Reliance on a third party for "nitty gritties." With a shell that has been developed by a third party, whether commercially or by another group in one's company, there is always the problem of what to do when bugs or inadequacies arise in the shell. Under the best of circumstances, the third party will be responsive to the knowledge engineer and do their best to either repair the damage to the shell or offer either another solution that addresses the inadequacy or a new release of the product. Under the worst of circumstances, the third party will have gone out of business, but it is also quite possible that they will be either unwilling or unable to make the necessary changes or suggestions.

Difficulties in tailoring a system for specific applications. Beyond the limitations imposed by using a generic knowledge representation scheme, there are always limits to the types of applications that can be built using a given structure or approach. When a purchaser is choosing a shell care must be exercised to ensure that it actually will conform to the application intended or to the range of applications intended if the purchaser is a developer of expert systems applications.

Alternatives to Shells

Beside the set of commercially available expert system shells, there are other tools and systems that can facilitate the development of expert systems. Each of the alternatives presumes that the expert system will be built from scratch and attempts to make that effort somewhat less difficult. Briefly, these can be categorized as follows:

Special-purpose languages. A number of high-level languages have been developed for the purpose of building expert systems, most notably OPS-5 and IRIS. Each of these languages contains the constructs and control structures that make the development of the expert system somewhat easier than it would be using LISP or Prolog.

Special-purpose hardware. As mentioned previously, computers dedicated to artificial intelligence programming have been developed. These machines include built-in development aids that are often of use to the developer of expert systems; however, they do not dedicate themselves to this type of application.

Special-purpose environment. One of the problems in developing expert systems from scratch is that a single language is usually chosen in which to implement the system, resulting in limitations of flexibility and/or performance as a result. There is a development environment that allows for the integration of each of the three artificial intelligence languages mentioned in this text with traditional languages. It is called Poplog, and was originally developed at the University of Sussex; it contains tutorials for the development of expert systems. Its availability is referenced in the notes for this chapter.

EXPERT SYSTEMS IN USE

There are a variety of expert systems in use today, the first having been developed in the 1970s. Many companies are reluctant to admit to their use of expert systems, especially in areas where such information could give their competitors proprietary information. Nonetheless, a number of systems have been widely publicized and serve as useful indicators of the types of expert systems that can be built with today's software technology.

Historic Systems

Mycin, a rule-based system developed in 1976 by Shortliffe, was designed to render advice as to the best type of medication to prescribe for bacterial infections in the blood. It employed backward chaining as its inference mechanism. Mycin's knowledge base was composed of a series of facts, each fact consisting of a set of lists, a variation of which is listed below.

In this representation, each fact consists of a pair of lists, referred to as the left hand side and right hand side. Each of these lists, with the exception of a single numeric value that appears on the right hand side, is organized into pairs of the type (attribute, value).

The strategy is that if all the pairs on the left hand side are true, then the attribute/value pair on the right hand side is true to the relative strength of the numeric value that appears on the right. The numbers themselves range between −1.0 and +1.0, where −1.0 corresponds with absolutely false, and +1.0 corresponds with absolutely true. Thus, a knowledge base written in Pop-11 might be expressed as follows:

```
[

[ [ [type mammal] [locomotion walking] [thumbs opposed] ]
    [ 1.0 [species human] ] ]

[ [ [type mammal] [locomotion crawling] [thumbs nonopposed] ]
    [ 0.5 [species dog] ] ]

[ [ [type mammal] [locomotion crawling] [thumbs nonopposed] ]
    [ 0.5 [species cat] ] ]

[ [ [type mammal] [locomotion swimming] [thumbs none] ]
    [ 1.0 [species dolphin] ] ]

[ [ [eggs internal] [covering hair] [nursing true] ]
    [ 1.0 [type mammal] ] ]

[ [ [eggs external] ]
    [ -1.0 [type mammal] ] ]

[ [ [eggs external] ]
    [ 1.0 [type bird] ] ]

[ [ [covering feathers] ]
    [ -1.0 [type mammal] ] ]

[ [ [covering feathers] ]
    [ 1.0 [type bird] ] ]

    ] -> knowledge_base
```

Prospector, another seminal expert system, was originally developed in 1978 by Duda at SRI International. This system, like that of Mycin, operated via backward chaining, this time to give advice about types of mineral deposits that were likely to be found underground, given certain information about the geologic structures of the region. It was particularly successful in that it managed to predict the presence of molybdenum at a site in Washington state, without the need for costly test drillings.

The structure of Prospector rules bears a strong resemblance to those in Mycin. Duda referred to them as inference rules rather than production rules, but in many ways the distinction is largely semantic. The primary difference was that Prospector looked for sets of known data that matched, to a better or worse degree, the set of data offered by the user. Furthermore, Prospector was able to recognize a user's set of data as being a subset of a larger case, which could lead to further questioning about the elements of the superset that were not mentioned initially by the user.

Modern Systems

A variety of expert systems are presently in use, some of which have been built with shells, others "from scratch." A look at representatives of each type yields an understanding of the typical differences between these systems and an appreciation for what can be accomplished using each approach.

Systems Built with Shells

One problem facing large computer companies is how to configure the hardware systems that their customers order. Depending on the specific needs of their customers, a variety of cables, interfaces, and other hardware will be required, all beyond the capabilities of the average salesperson to remain current on. Two large systems have been built for this purpose, one for DEC and the other for ICL, a large British computer company. DEC's system was written long before the advent of expert system shells and has grown so large that it requires a significant number of programmers to remain on a maintenance team full time. ICL's program, called Dragon, was built with a shell and thus has proved to be much more maintainable.

Banks often have a variety of rules, policies, and procedures to help them determine eligibility for their financial products. A system was developed to enable a group of banks to help their employees determine whether or not an applicant for a mortgage was qualified for the mortgage. This system also gave advice as to what conditions should be imposed, and what rate should be granted.

The petroleum industry has been one of the most dedicated users of expert systems, beginning with Prospector. A more recent example is a system designed to help with the decision as to whether to invest in third-world countries, examining various factors to help predict the likelihood of political unrest, overthrow of the government, attack from neighbors, and other deleterious events.

Another complicated task is that of designing and maintaining telephone networks: the quantity of information about cabling, routes, and loads quickly becomes so high that, while it is easy to understand in principle, it becomes impossible to manage on any realistic basis. A system was built for use by the British telephone industry to help with that task, providing advice on set-up and fault diagnosis for their larger telephone exchanges.

Systems Built without Shells

As mentioned earlier, an expert system was built to function as a real-time assistant to air traffic controllers. The problems of air traffic control are quite complex: the controller must respond quickly to a number of different types of information, including weather, paths that planes are taking, overall congestion, and *rogue* (or unexpected) aircraft. Furthermore, the controller cannot depend on his or her instructions being followed precisely, either due to poor transmission, changing conditions of the weather or aircraft involved, or simple misunderstanding. Thus, the controller must endeavor to anticipate serious problems long before they occur, so that pilots need not respond in such a tight time frame.

The system that was built was designed to operate in real time, during those periods when the controller would most need assistance; that is, when the skies are full of aircraft. The system was further designed to operate with the same constraints as the human controller, in that it was not assumed that the controller would always take the system's advice, and as such the system had to learn from its interaction with the human controller. The final system went from the proof-of-concept stage into simulation with real-time data, but was never implemented, presumably due to concerns by the human controllers about yielding any of their decision-making power to a computer.

Another system, which also functioned in real time, was built to help with a large security system. The difficulty here was that due to the large number and high sensitivity of the intrusion detection devices, a high percentage of false alarms was being recorded. The expert system used a "learning" algorithm that took in data from the sensors, combined it with reports as to the validity of any reported intrusions, and from that data generated a system of rules that dramatically reduced the number of false alarms.

One problem facing the aerospace industry is the identification of unfamiliar objects from various real-time data. This data is often "noisy," in that it has been corrupted either by natural phenomena, faulty equipment, or deliberate attempts to jam the receiving equipment. This noisy data must be matched against known parameters, any one of which will probably be insufficient for clear identification. This task becomes even more complex when the identification must take place in real time. A system was built to accomplish this task and successfully implemented overseas.

You will notice that the systems built from scratch exhibit a greater amount of control over the interactions with the real world, particularly in their ability to process real-time data. Furthermore, they have a richer structure of rules, and as such would be difficult at best to implement using an expert system shell.

The examples built using a shell, however, were developed in what is estimated would be one third to one half of the time required for similar systems built without a shell. Information regarding obtaining the specifics of these systems can be found in the notes for this chapter.

SUMMARY

Expert systems have found their way into the commercial world, although at present they have really only just arrived. There are a variety of applications that appear to be suited to expert systems and a corresponding variety of tools to build them with. As the notion of a computerized adviser becomes more commonplace, it will be likely that the somewhat hyperbolic term *expert system* will disappear, and much of the resistance to using these systems along with it. The crucial notion here is that expert systems and their descendents can do much the same thing for people that computers can do: eliminate much of the drudgery and dangerous work from our lives, but never replace us.

Notes

CHAPTER 1

Colby, K.M., *Artificial Paranoia*, New York: Pergammon Press, 1975.

Faught, W.S., Colby, K.M., and Parkinson, R., *The interaction of inferences, affects, and intentions in a model of paranoia. Memo AIM-253,* Stanford Artificial Intelligence Laboratory, Stanford University, 1974.

Hart, P.E., Duda, R.O., and Einaudi, M.T., *PROSPECTOR—a computer-based consultation system for mineral exploration. Mathematical Geology,* vol. 10, no. 5, 1978.

Shortliffe, E.H., *MYCIN: computer based medical consultations.* New York: Elsevier, 1976.

Waltz, D.L., *Scientific DataLink's artificial intelligence classification scheme. The A.I. Magazine,* Spring 1985, pp. 58-63.

Weizenbaum, J., *ELIZA—a computer program for the study of natural language communication between man and machine. Communications of the ACM,* vol. 9, no. 1, pp. 36-45.

Winston, P.H., *Artificial Intelligence (second edition).* Reading, MA: Addison-Wesley, 1984.

Winston, P.H., and Pendergast, K.A. (editors), *The AI business—commercial uses of artificial intelligence.* Cambridge, MA: MIT Press, 1984.

CHAPTER 2

Brule, J.F., *Fuzzy Logic—a tutorial. Proceedings of the First Hartford Graduate Center Computer Science Conference,* 1985.

CHAPTER 4

Nilsson, N.J., *Principles of artificial intelligence.* Palo Alto, CA: Tioga Publishing Co., 1980.

CHAPTER 5

Barrett, R., Ramsay, A., Sloman, A., *Pop-11: a practical language for artificial intelligence.* New York: John Wiley and Sons, 1985.

Burstall, R.M., Collins, J.S., Popplestone, R.J., *Programming in Pop-2.* Edinburgh University Press, 1971.

Clocksin, W.F., Mellish, C.S., *Programming in Prolog.* 2nd edition, New York: Springer-Verlag, 1984.

Winston, P.H., Horn, B.K.P., *LISP*, 2nd edition, Reading MA: Addison-Wesley, 1984.

CHAPTER 7

Rosenblatt, F., *The perceptron: a perceiving and recognizing automaton.* Ithaca NY: Cornell Univ., Project PARA, Cornell Aeronaut. Lab. Rep., 85-460-1, 1957.

Wong, A.K.C., and You, M. *Entropy and distance of random graphs with application to structural pattern recognition. IEEE Transactions Pattern Analysis and Machine Intelligence,* Vol. PAMI-7, no. 5, pp. 559-609, 1985.

CHAPTER 9

Barr, A., and Feigenbaum, E.A., MYCIN. In *The handbook of artificial intelligence*, vol., II, William Kaufman, Inc., Los Altos, CA, 1982.

Duda, R.O., Gashnig, J., Hart, P.E., Konolige, K., Reboh, R., Barrett, P., and Slocum, J., *Development of the PROSPECTOR consultation system for mineral exploration,* Final report, SRI projects 5821 and 6415. Menlo Park, CA: SRI International, Inc., 1978.

Shortliffe, E.H., Computer-based medical consultations: MYCIN. *American* New York: Elsevier, 1976.

POPLOG, available in North America through Systems Designers Software Inc., 444 Washington St., Woburn MA 01801. European Office: Systems Designers plc, 1 Pembroke Broadway, Camberley, Surrey, England.

(All of the examples of expert system design without the use of a shell in this chapter were developed using the Poplog system, referenced above. The shell used in each of the four "shell" examples was Envisage, produced by the companies that produced Poplog.)

FURTHER READING

Edward Feigenbaum and Julian Feldman, eds., *Computers and Thought,* McGraw-Hill, New York, 1963.

Artificial Intelligence: Theory, Logic and Application

Philip Jackson, Jr., *Introduction to Artificial Intelligence*, Petrocelli/Charter, New York, 1974.

Nils J. Nilsson, *Problem-Solving Methods in Artificial Intelligence*, McGraw-Hill, New York, 1971.

Bertram Raphael, *The Thinking Computer*, W.H. Freeman, San Francisco, 1976.

James R. Slagel, *Artificial Intelligence: The Heuristic Programming Approach*, McGraw-Hill, New York, 1971.

Patrick Henry Winston, *Artificial Intelligence*, Addison-Wesley, Reading, Mass., 1977.

Index

Index

Edited by Marilyn L. Johnson

Other Bestsellers From TAB

☐ **LEARNING C WITH TINY-C**

Have the power, flexibility, and convenience of C . . . for a fraction of the cost of a compiler! All you need is this hands-on guide and the tiny-c interpreter (supplied on disk with book). In fact, by the end of chapter one, you should be able to write, debug, and run tiny-c programs and build software systems based on these programs . . . it's as easy as that! 176 pp., 12 illus. 7" × 10". Paperback. Includes disk for IBM PC® with 128 K.

Paper $34.90   **Book No. 5160**

☐ **LISP—THE LANGUAGE OF ARTIFICIAL INTELLIGENCE—Holtz**

Now here's your opportunity to learn and use LISP . . . to enter the realm of artificial intelligence with confidence. Holtz explains LISP vocabulary and how artificial intelligence programming concepts differ. You'll get a look at how LISP handles mathematical operations . . . be introduced to logical operators . . . and see how close BASIC input/output is to that of Common LISP. 272 pp., 7" × 10".

Paper $16.95   **Hard $25.95**
Book No. 2620

☐ **ARTIFICIAL INTELLIGENCE PROJECTS FOR THE COMMODORE 64™**

This uniquely-exciting guide includes: 16 ready-to-run, fully-explained projects, illustrating a wide variety of artificial intelligence techniques; a plain-English introduction to artificial intelligence, robotics, and LISP; a complete glossary of artificial intelligence terminology; easy-to-follow examples and show-how illustrations; plus a quick-look-up index for fast reference. 160 pp., 15 illus. 7" × 10".

Paper $12.95   **Book No. 1883**

☐ **ROBOTICS—Cardoza and Vlk**

This comprehensive overview traces the historical progression of robotics and the enormous impact robots are making on our society. Includes a look at opportunities and a listing of schools and training programs. Plus, a large comprehensive glossary of robotics terms, a complete bibliography of helpful books, magazines, and information sources, and a listing of the robots now on the market including their manufacturers. 160 pp., 28 illus. 7" × 10".

Paper $10.95   **Hard $16.95**
Book No. 1858

☐ **DESIGNING AND PROGRAMMING PERSONAL EXPERT SYSTEMS—Townsend and Feucht**

Discover how new trends in artificial intelligence (AI) concepts can be put to practical use on almost any personal computer including the Apple® II or IBM® PC! Explore expert system programming techniques that can be modified or enhanced to create your own system for electronics, engineering, or other technical applications! It's all here for the taking in this exciting and challenging new sourcebook! 250 pp., 75 illus. Large Format. (7" × 10").

Paper $18.95   **Hard $27.95**
Book No. 2692

☐ **THE PERSONAL ROBOT BOOK**

This state-of-the-art "buyer's guide" fills you in on all the details for buying or building your own and even how to interface a robot with your personal computer! Illustrated with dozens of actual photographs, it features details on all the newest models now available on the market. Ideal for the hobbyist who wants to get more involved in robotics without getting in over his head. 192 pp., 105 illus. 7" × 10".

Paper $12.95   **Hard $21.95**
Book No. 1896

☐ **SUREFIRE PROGRAMMING IN C—Stewart**

Using plenty of illustrated, step-by-step examples, you'll ease right through such important concepts in C programming as compile and link commands, C input and output, arrays; character strings, formal parameters, arithmetic and relational operators, and even advanced topics. Turn to this step-by-step beginner's guide and begin taking advantage of the power of C right away! 288 pp., 55 illus. 7" × 10". Printed in Two-Color.

Paper $16.95   **Hard $21.95**
Book No. 1873

☐ **BEGINNING FORTH—Chirlian**

Thorough and easy-to-follow, this guide to FORTH provides you with all the commands, operations, statements, and program writing advice you'll need to fully understand and use this powerful language's potential. You'll find: a comparison of FORTH with other programming languages; step-by-step explanations of disk operations; fundamental concepts of structured programming; even a FORTH glossary. 256 pp., 7" × 10".

Hard $24.95   **Book No. 1822**

Other Bestsellers From TAB

Other Bestsellers From TAB

☐ **THE ILLUSTRATED
DICTIONARY OF MICROCOMPUTERS—2nd Edition**

Little more than a decade after the introduction of the first microprocessors, microcomputers have made a major impact on every area of today's business, industry, and personal lifestyles. The result: a whole new language of terms and concepts reflecting this rapidly developing technology . . . and a vital need for current, accurate explanations of what these terms and concepts mean. Michael Hordeski has provided just that in this completely revised and greatly expanded new second edition of *The Illustrated Dictionary of Microcomputers*! 368 pp., 357 illus. Large, Desk-Top Format (7″ × 10″).

Paper $14.95
Book No. 2688   **Hard $24.95**

☐ **FORTH: The Fourth-Generation Language**

Using dozens of detailed illustrations and example programs, the author leads off with an examination of the unique structure of FORTH and its applications potential. Then you'll get hands-on instructions in using the system stack, data storage on the stack, data storage in variables, parameter passing on the stack, creating new command words, manipulating disk blocks, and the use of control structures to change program flow. With the mastery of these fundamentals, you'll be ready to start creating programs to solve specific problems that are particularly adaptable to the style, clarity and efficiency offered by the FORTH language. 192 pp., 116 illus. Large Format (7″ × 10″).

Paper $18.95
Book No. 2687   **Hard $26.95**

DATE DUE